by Bryan Talbot

DARK HORSE BOOKS®

For Alwyn

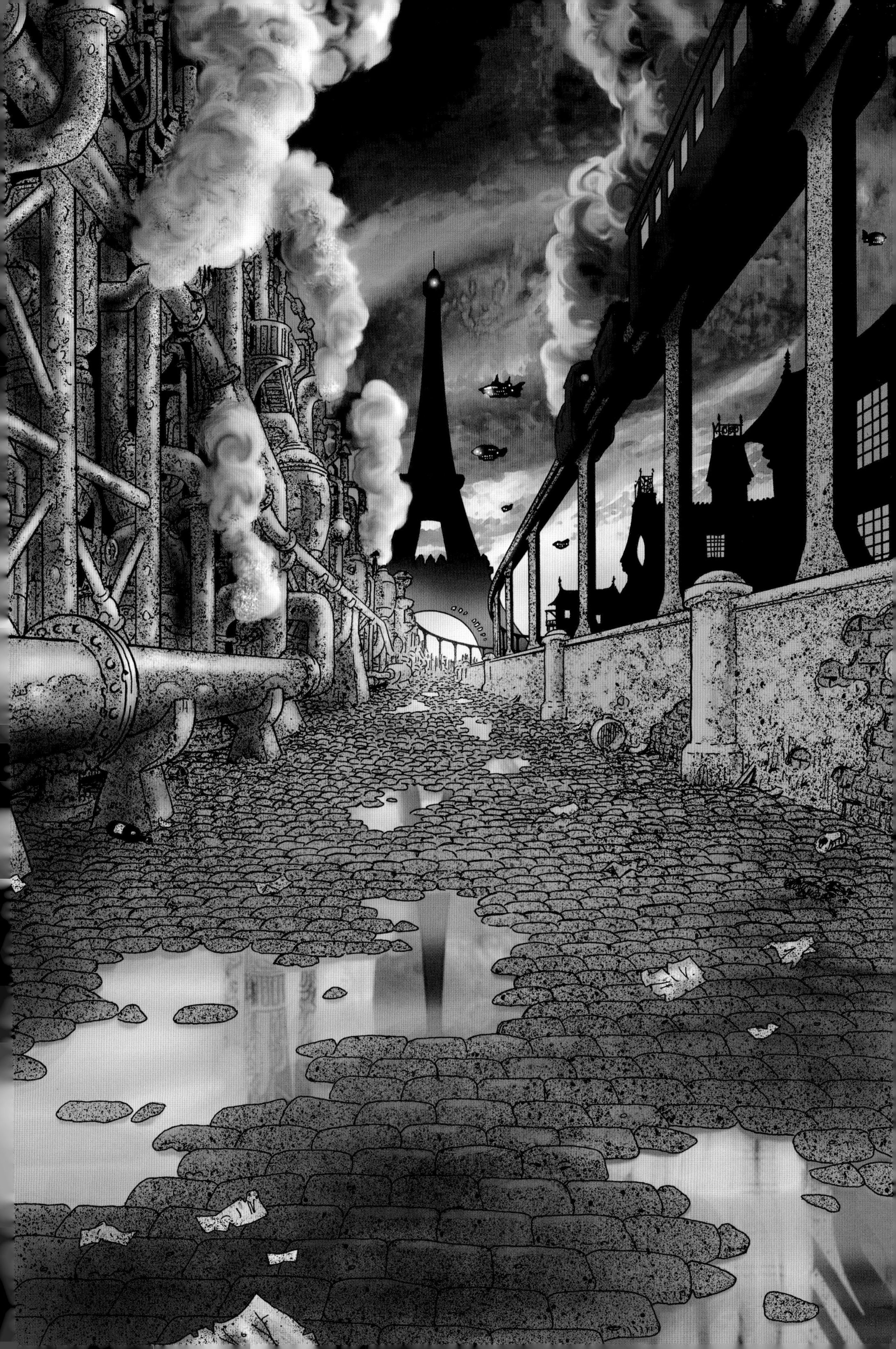

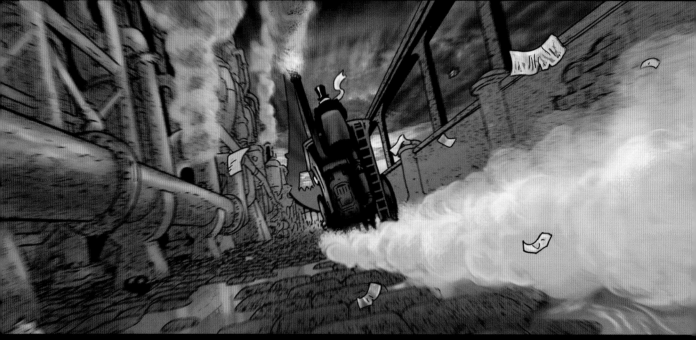

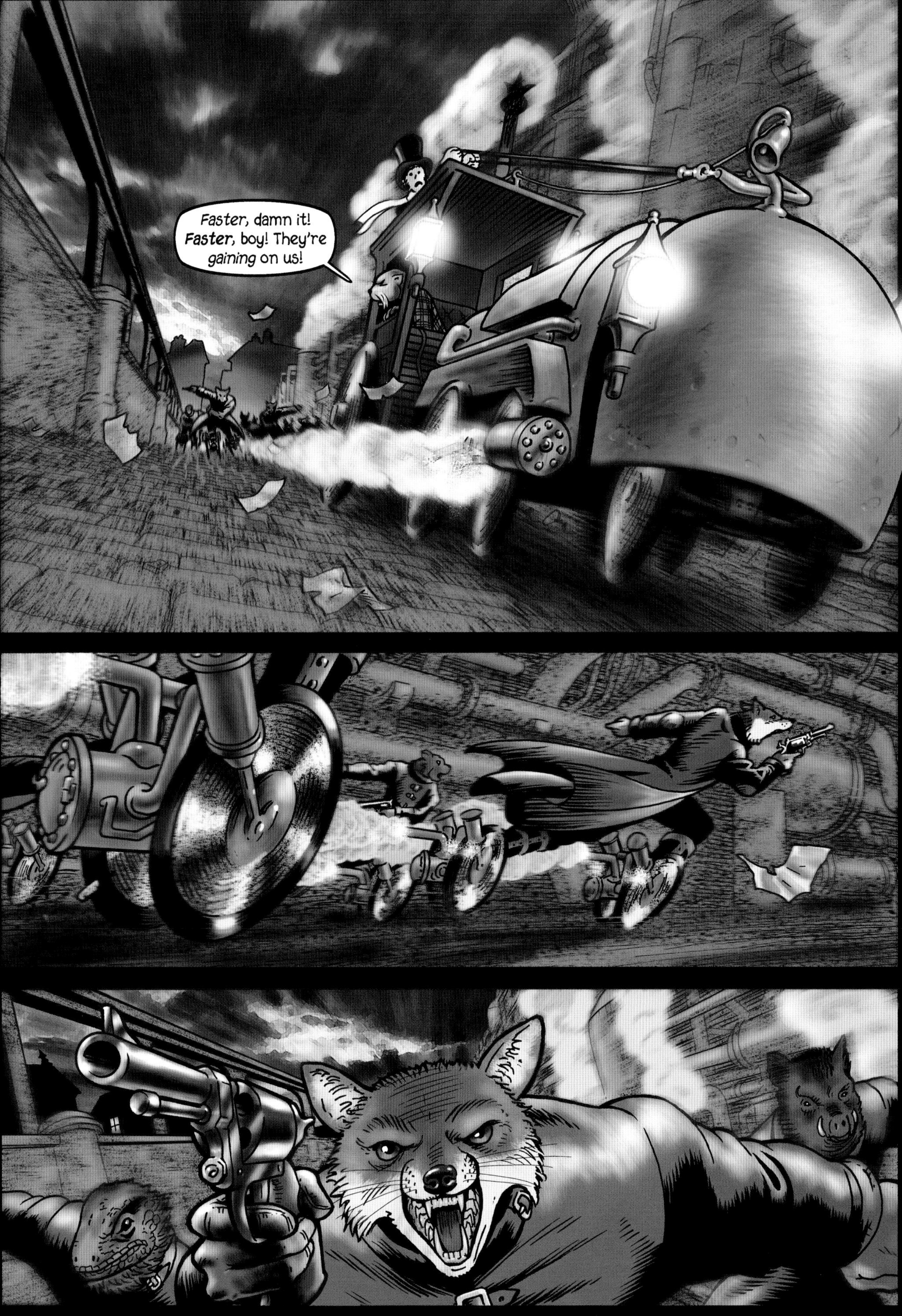
Faster, damn it! Faster, boy! They're gaining on us!

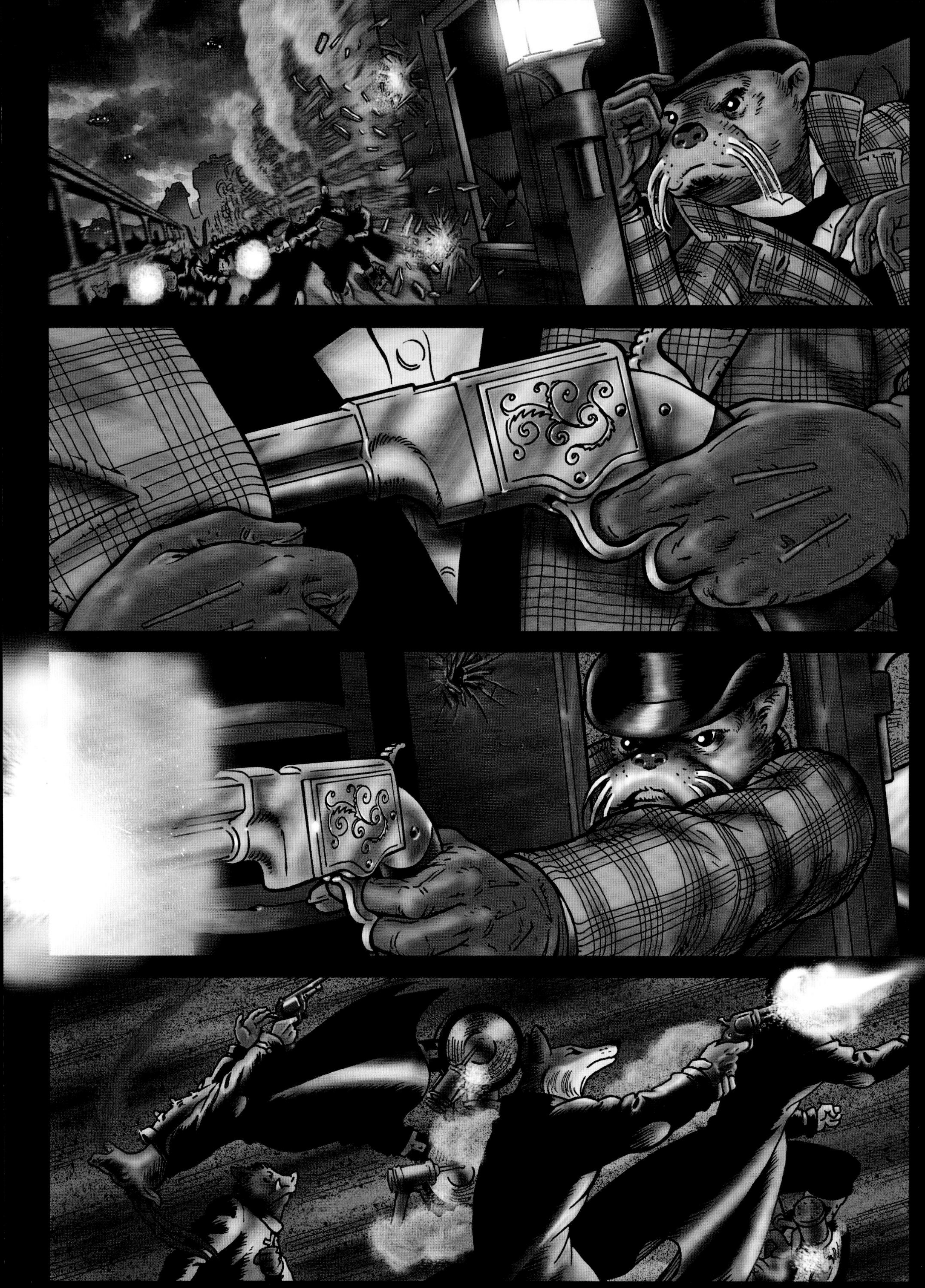

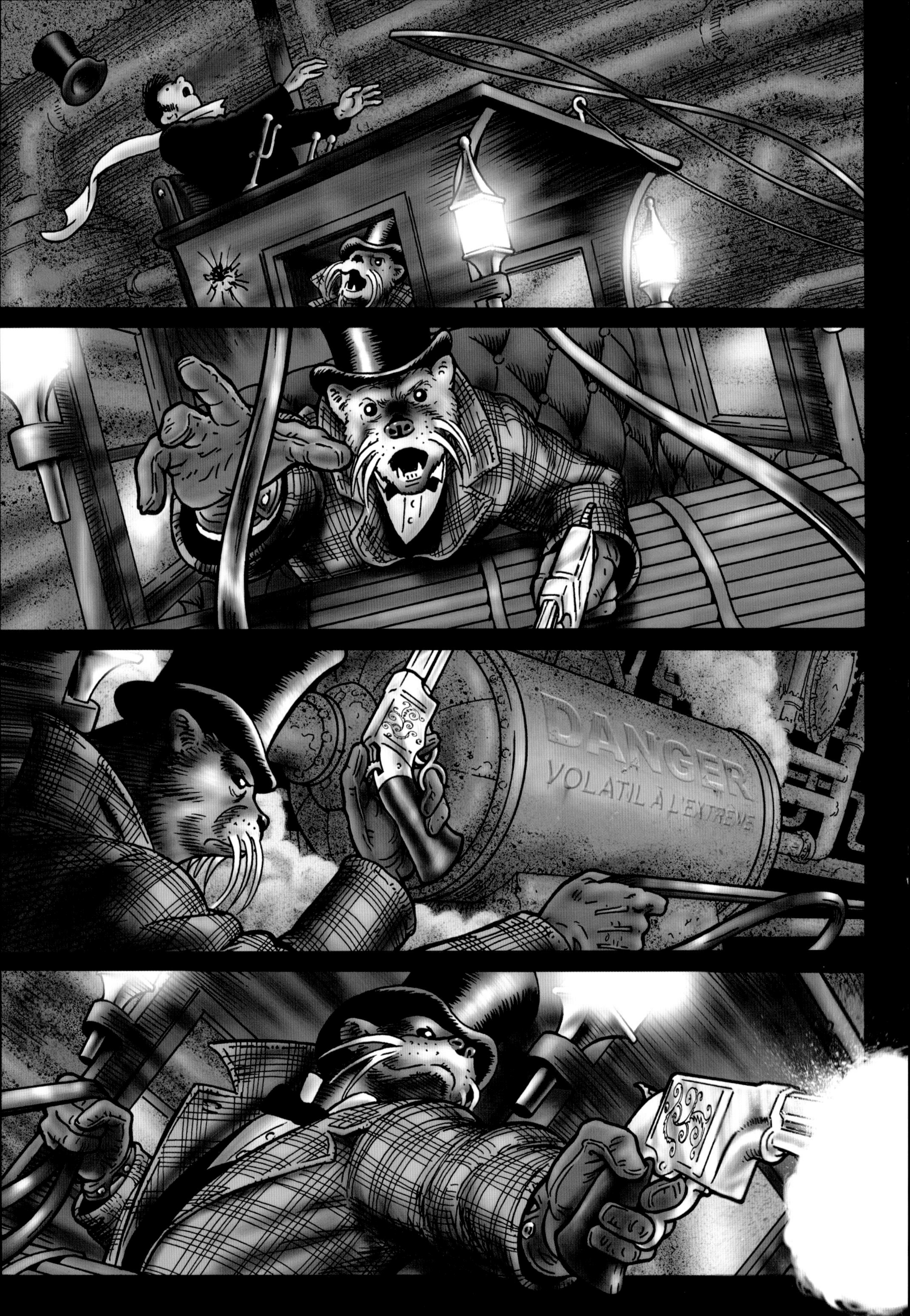
DANGER
VOLATIL À L'EXTRÊME

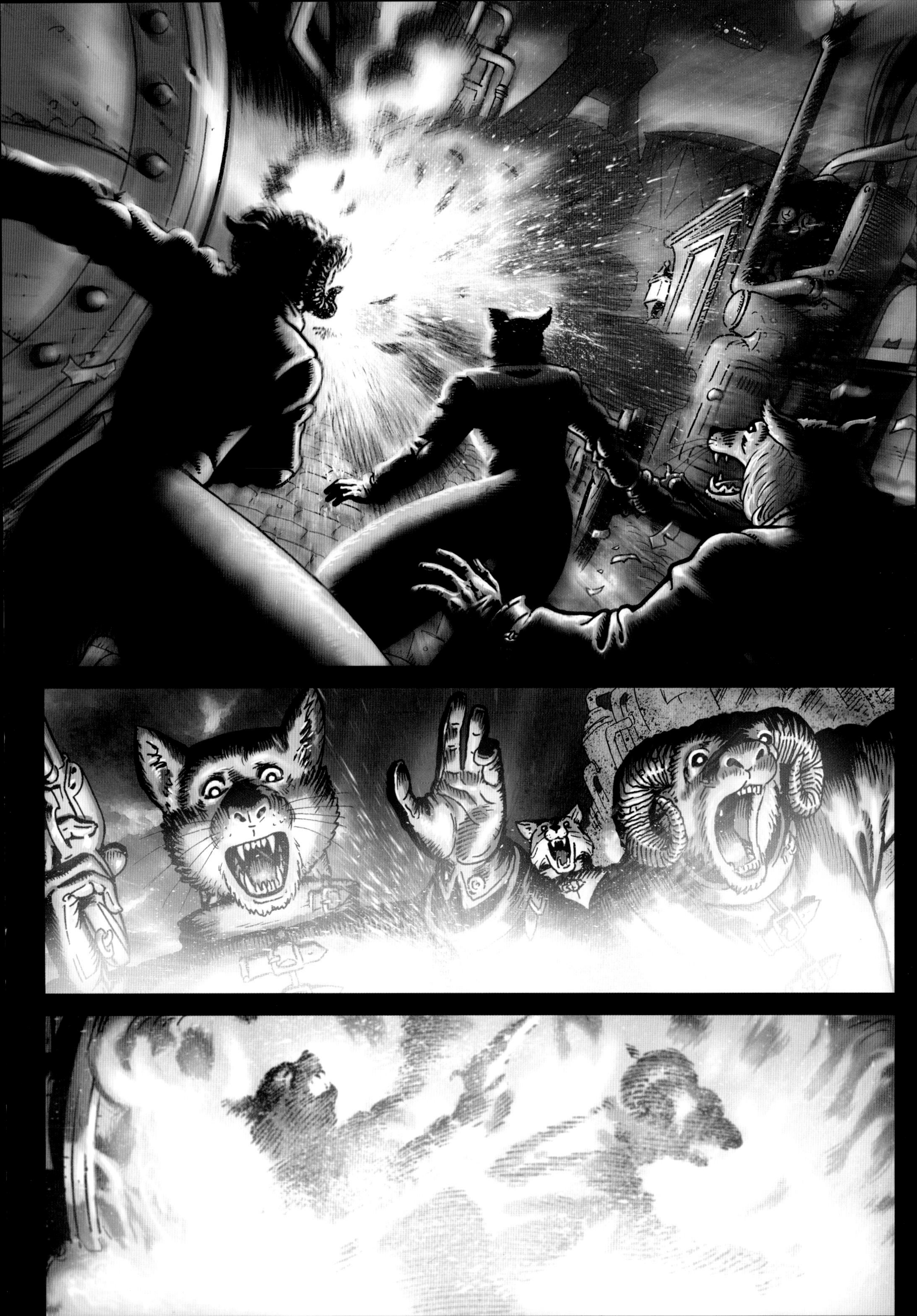

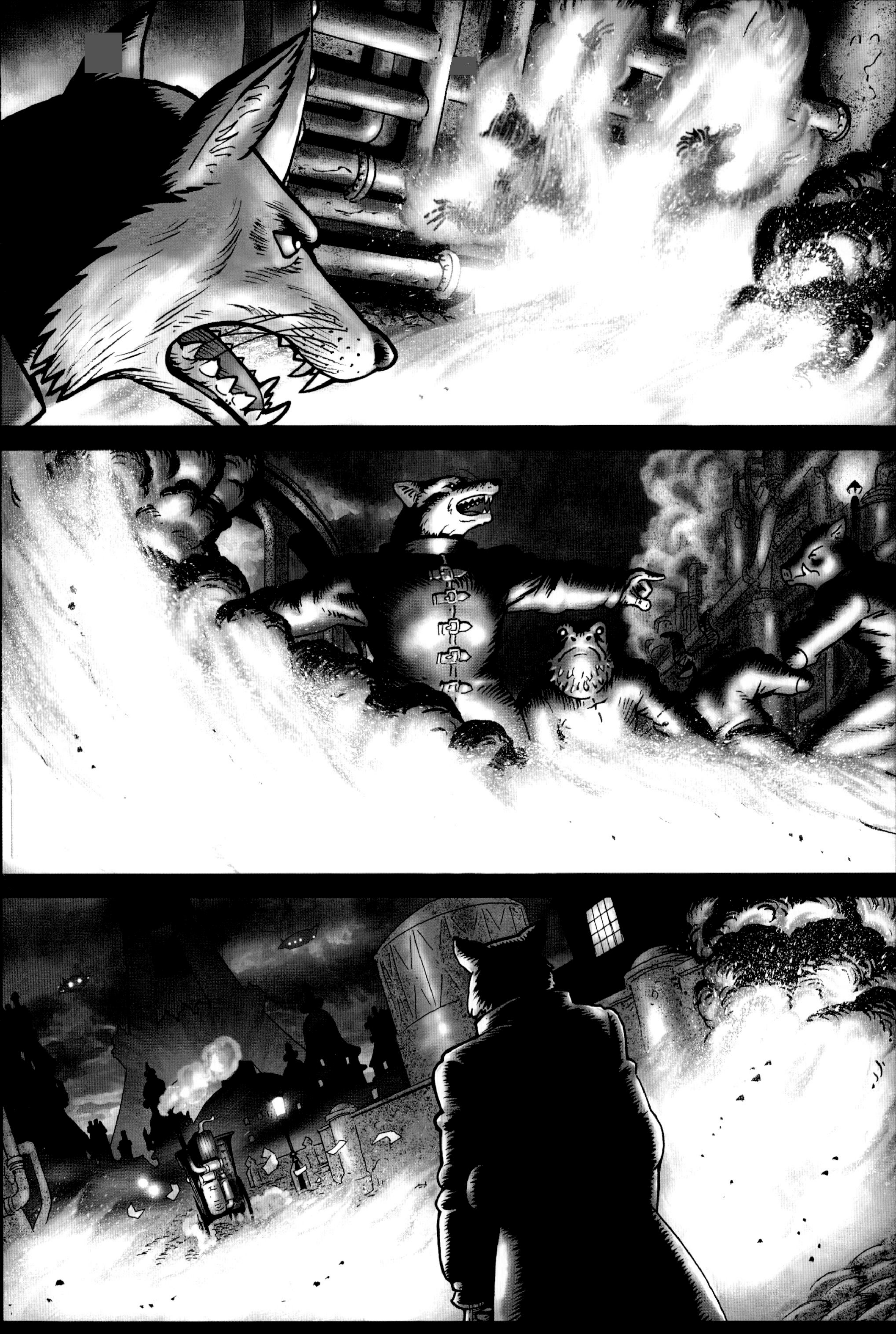

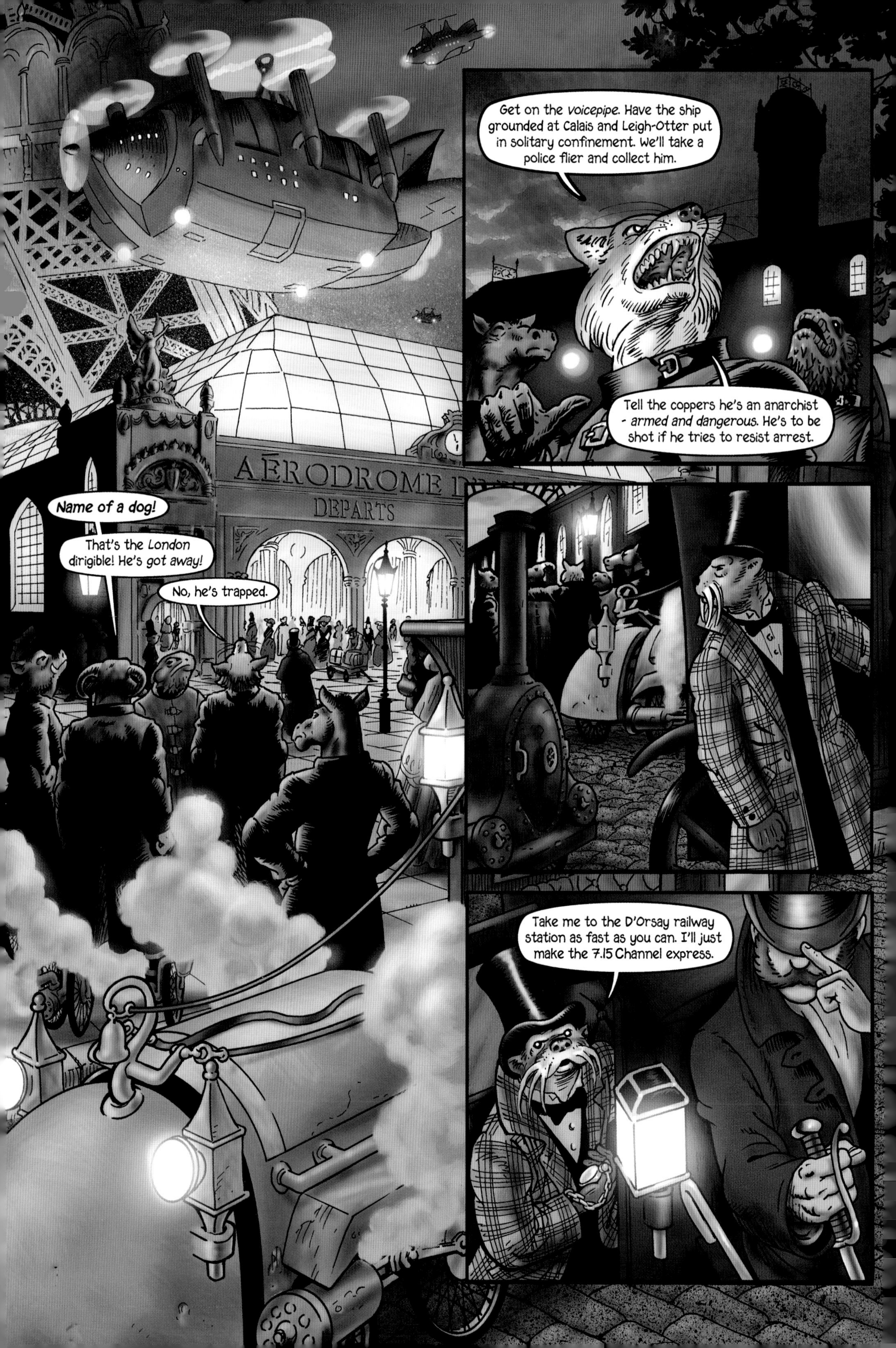
AÉRODROME D
DEPARTS
Name of a dog!
That's the London dirigible! He's got away!
No, he's trapped.
Get on the voicepipe. Have the ship grounded at Calais and Leigh-Otter put in solitary confinement. We'll take a police flier and collect him.
Tell the coppers he's an anarchist - armed and dangerous. He's to be shot if he tries to resist arrest.
Take me to the D'Orsay railway station as fast as you can. I'll just make the 7.15 Channel express.

A Fantasy

by
Bryan Talbot

Script, art & book design: Bryan Talbot

This story was inspired by the work of
the French caricaturist Jean Ignace Isidore Gérard (1803–1847),
who worked under the nom de plume J. J. Grandville,
and the seminal science - fiction illustrator,
fellow Frenchman Albert Robida (1848–1926)

Not to mention Sir Arthur Conan Doyle, Rupert the Bear,
and Quentin Tarantino

Bryan Talbot lettering font produced by Comicraft
Colour flats pages 26 – 98: Jordan Smith
French Advisor: Marie-Paul Brown

Art Nouveau steampunk pattern by Bryan Talbot,
based on the endpapers of "Dampf und Elektricität:
die Technik im Anfange des XX Jahrhunderts."
Berlin: W. Herlet. [c. 1900]

Sincere acknowledgements for proof-reading,
comments on the work-in-progress, and other important input to
Chaz Brenchley, Eric Bufkens, Dan Franklin, Nat Gertler, Dr. Mel Gibson,
Paul Gravett, Jordan Smith, Dr. Mary Talbot, Sylvie Toll, and Chris Warner

No animals were harmed in the making of this book

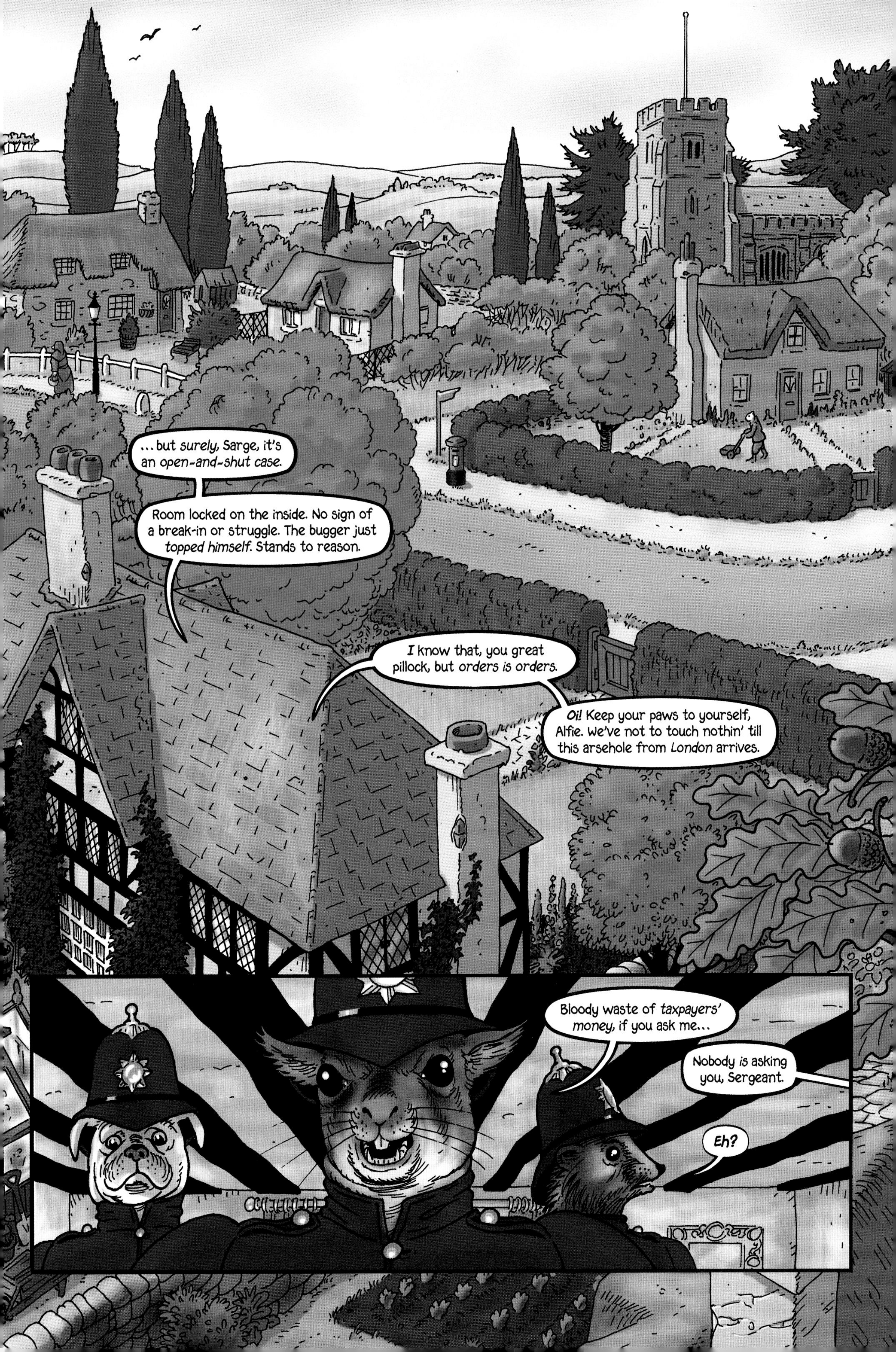
...but surely, Sarge, it's an open-and-shut case.
Room locked on the inside. No sign of a break-in or struggle. The bugger just topped himself. Stands to reason.
I know that, you great pillock, but orders is orders.
Oi! Keep your paws to yourself, Alfie. We've not to touch nothin' till this arsehole from London arrives.
Bloody waste of taxpayers' money, if you ask me...
Nobody is asking you, Sergeant.
Eh?

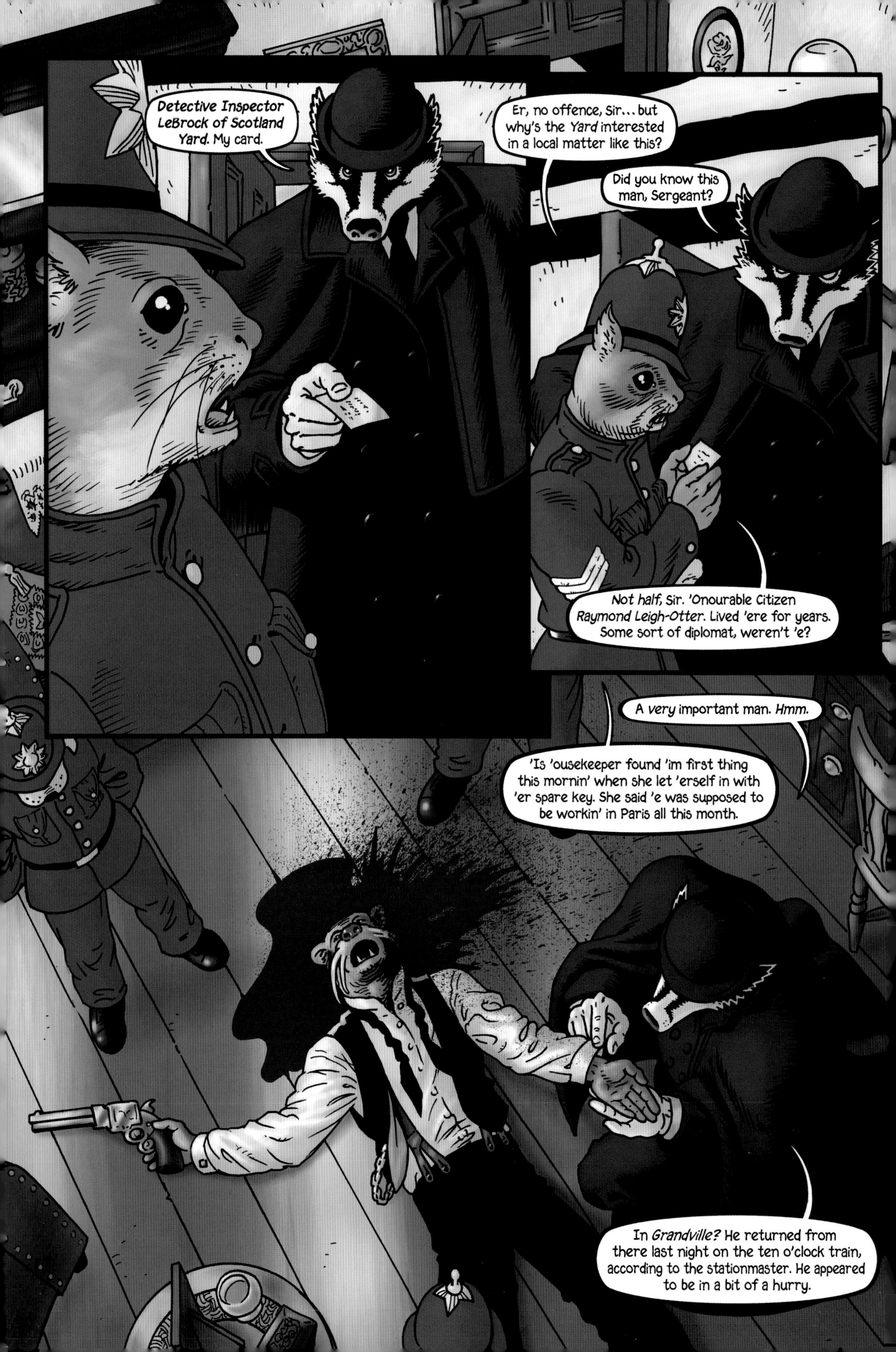
Detective Inspector LeBrock of Scotland Yard. My card.
Er, no offence, Sir... but why's the Yard interested in a local matter like this?
Did you know this man, Sergeant?
Not half, Sir. 'Onourable Citizen Raymond Leigh-Otter. Lived 'ere for years. Some sort of diplomat, weren't 'e?
A very important man. Hmm.
'Is 'ousekeeper found 'im first thing this mornin' when she let 'erself in with 'er spare key. She said 'e was supposed to be workin' in Paris all this month.
In Grandville? He returned from there last night on the ten o'clock train, according to the stationmaster. He appeared to be in a bit of a hurry.

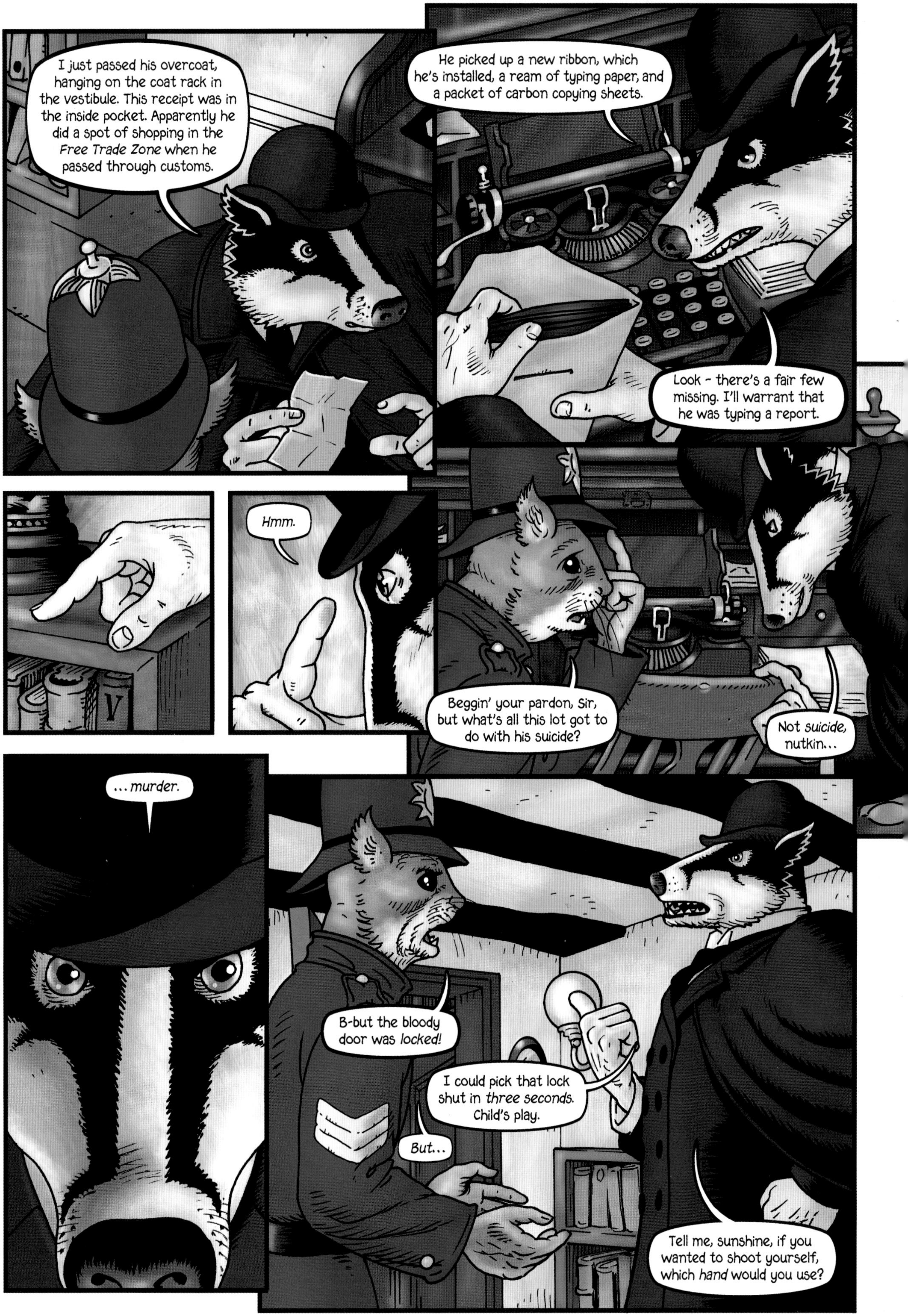

I just passed his overcoat, hanging on the coat rack in the vestibule. This receipt was in the inside pocket. Apparently he did a spot of shopping in the *Free Trade Zone* when he passed through customs.
He picked up a new ribbon, which he's installed, a ream of typing paper, and a packet of carbon copying sheets.
Look - there's a fair few missing. I'll warrant that he was typing a report.
Hmm.
Beggin' your pardon, Sir, but what's all this lot got to do with his suicide?
Not *suicide*, nutkin...
...*murder*.
B-but the bloody door was *locked*!
I could pick that lock shut in *three seconds*. Child's play.
But...
Tell me, sunshine, if you wanted to shoot yourself, which *hand* would you use?

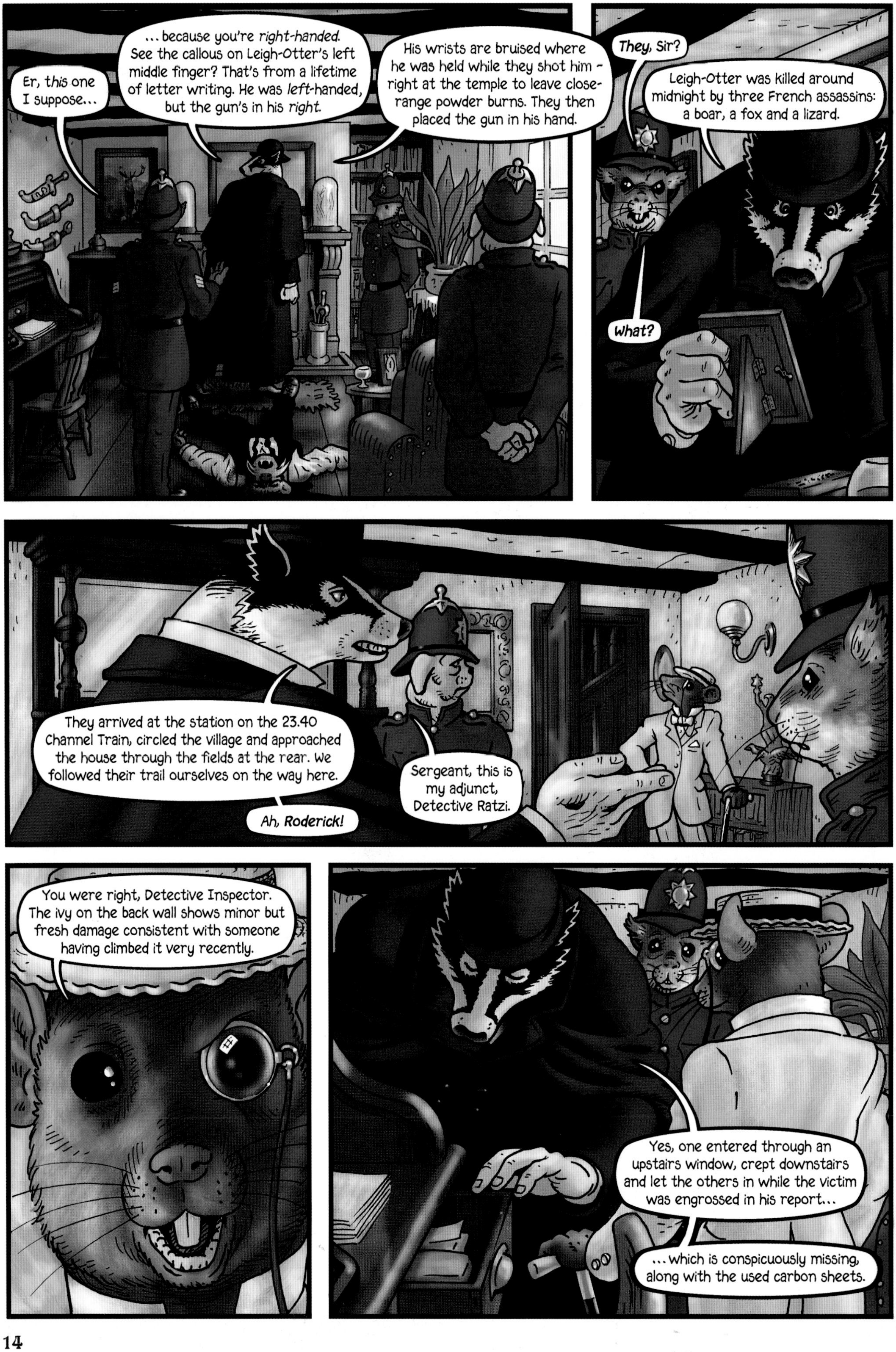
Er, this one I suppose...
...because you're right-handed. See the callous on Leigh-Otter's left middle finger? That's from a lifetime of letter writing. He was left-handed, but the gun's in his right.
His wrists are bruised where he was held while they shot him - right at the temple to leave close-range powder burns. They then placed the gun in his hand.
They, Sir?
Leigh-Otter was killed around midnight by three French assassins: a boar, a fox and a lizard.
What?
They arrived at the station on the 23.40 Channel Train, circled the village and approached the house through the fields at the rear. We followed their trail ourselves on the way here.
Ah, Roderick!
Sergeant, this is my adjunct, Detective Ratzi.
You were right, Detective Inspector. The ivy on the back wall shows minor but fresh damage consistent with someone having climbed it very recently.
Yes, one entered through an upstairs window, crept downstairs and let the others in while the victim was engrossed in his report...
...which is conspicuously missing, along with the used carbon sheets.

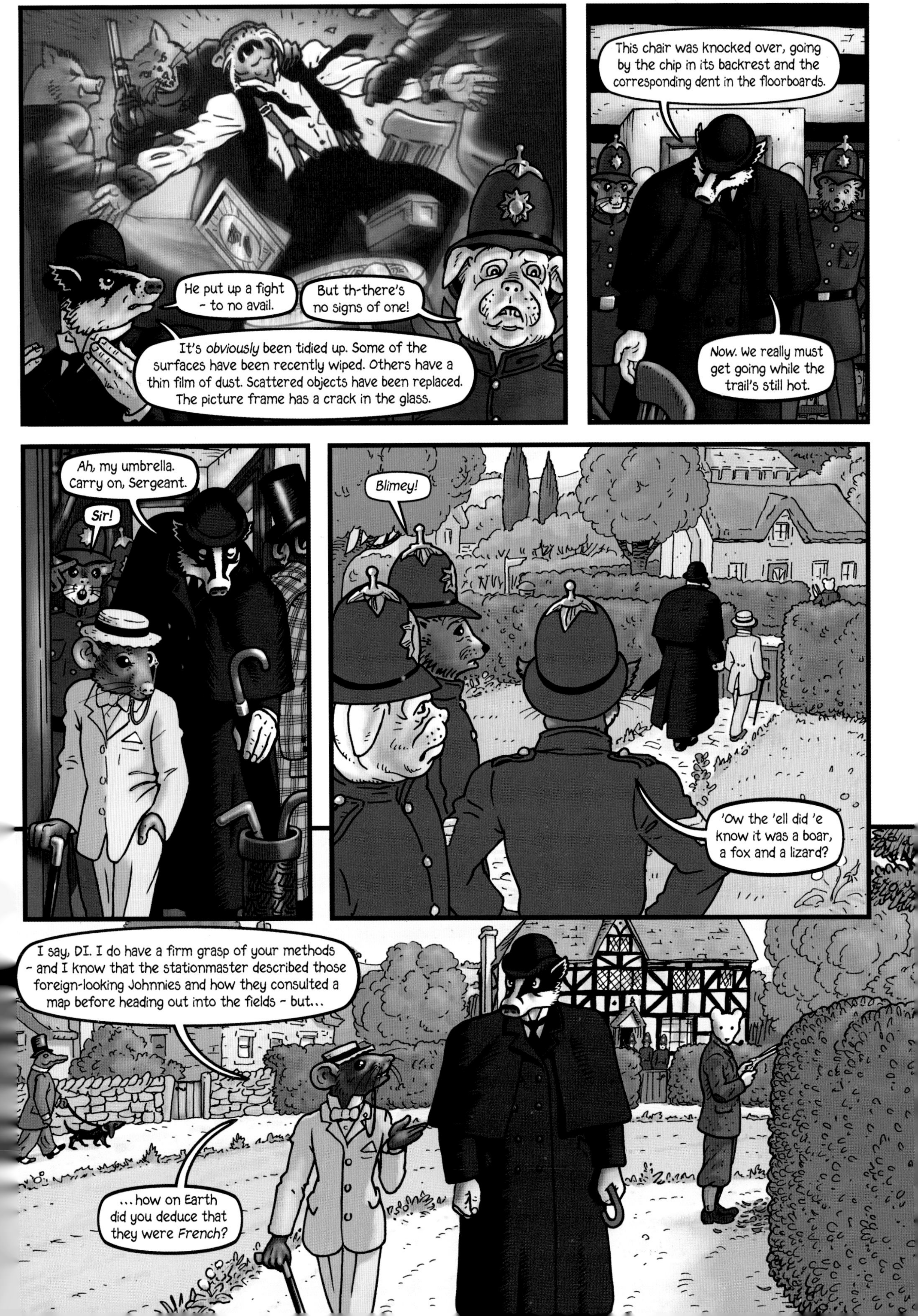

He put up a fight - to no avail.
But th-there's no signs of one!
It's *obviously* been tidied up. Some of the surfaces have been recently wiped. Others have a thin film of dust. Scattered objects have been replaced. The picture frame has a crack in the glass.
This chair was knocked over, going by the chip in its backrest and the corresponding dent in the floorboards.
Now. We really must get going while the trail's still hot.
Ah, my umbrella. Carry on, Sergeant.
Sir!
Blimey!
'Ow the 'ell did 'e know it was a boar, a fox and a lizard?
I say, DI. I do have a firm grasp of your methods - and I know that the stationmaster described those foreign-looking Johnnies and how they consulted a map before heading out into the fields - but...
...how on Earth did you deduce that they were *French*?

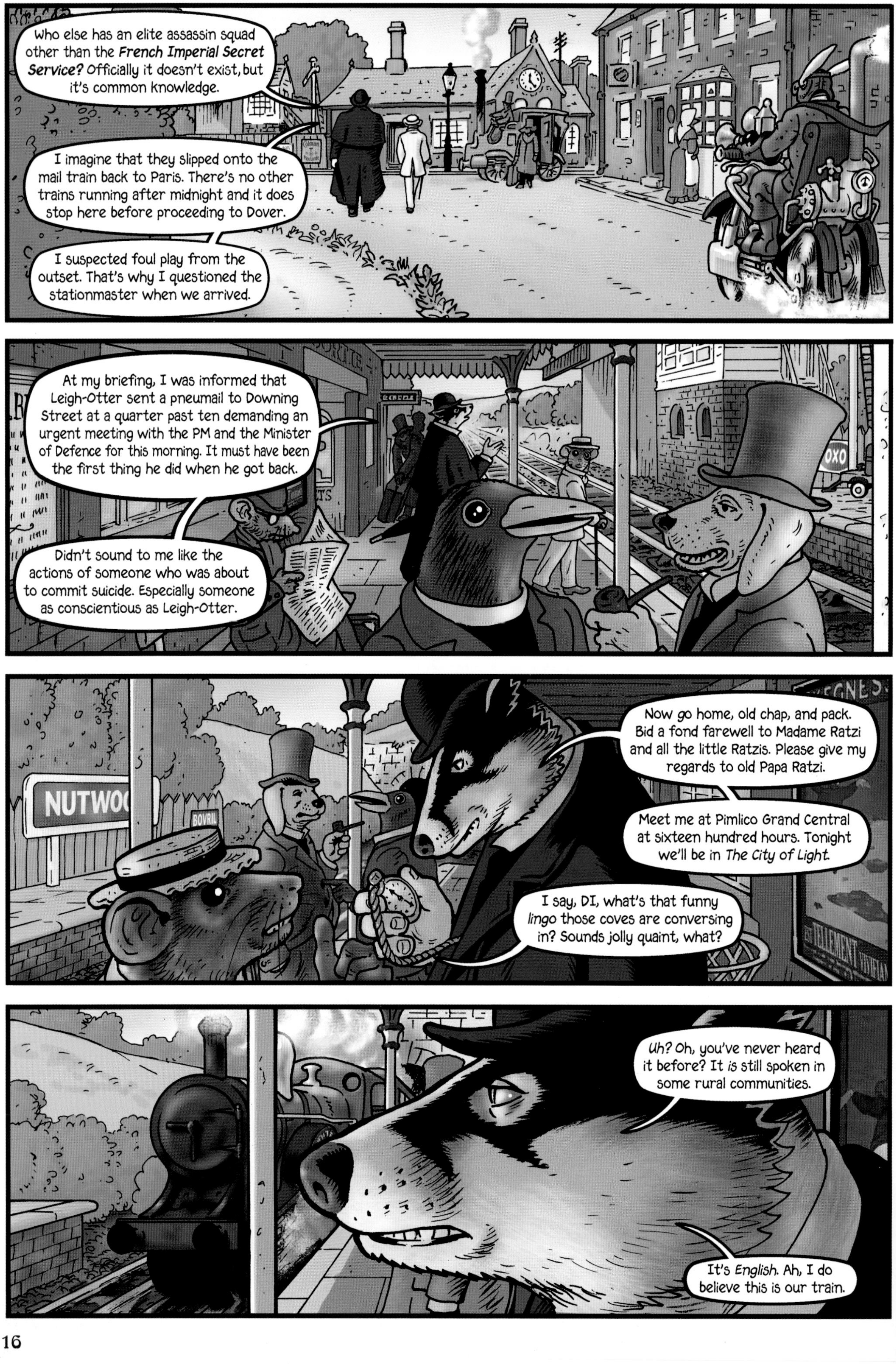
Who else has an elite assassin squad other than the French Imperial Secret Service? Officially it doesn't exist, but it's common knowledge.
I imagine that they slipped onto the mail train back to Paris. There's no other trains running after midnight and it does stop here before proceeding to Dover.
I suspected foul play from the outset. That's why I questioned the stationmaster when we arrived.
At my briefing, I was informed that Leigh-Otter sent a pneumail to Downing Street at a quarter past ten demanding an urgent meeting with the PM and the Minister of Defence for this morning. It must have been the first thing he did when he got back.
Didn't sound to me like the actions of someone who was about to commit suicide. Especially someone as conscientious as Leigh-Otter.
OXO
NUTWOO
BOVRIL
Now go home, old chap, and pack. Bid a fond farewell to Madame Ratzi and all the little Ratzis. Please give my regards to old Papa Ratzi.
Meet me at Pimlico Grand Central at sixteen hundred hours. Tonight we'll be in The City of Light.
I say, DI, what's that funny lingo those coves are conversing in? Sounds jolly quaint, what?
Uh? Oh, you've never heard it before? It is still spoken in some rural communities.
It's English. Ah, I do believe this is our train.

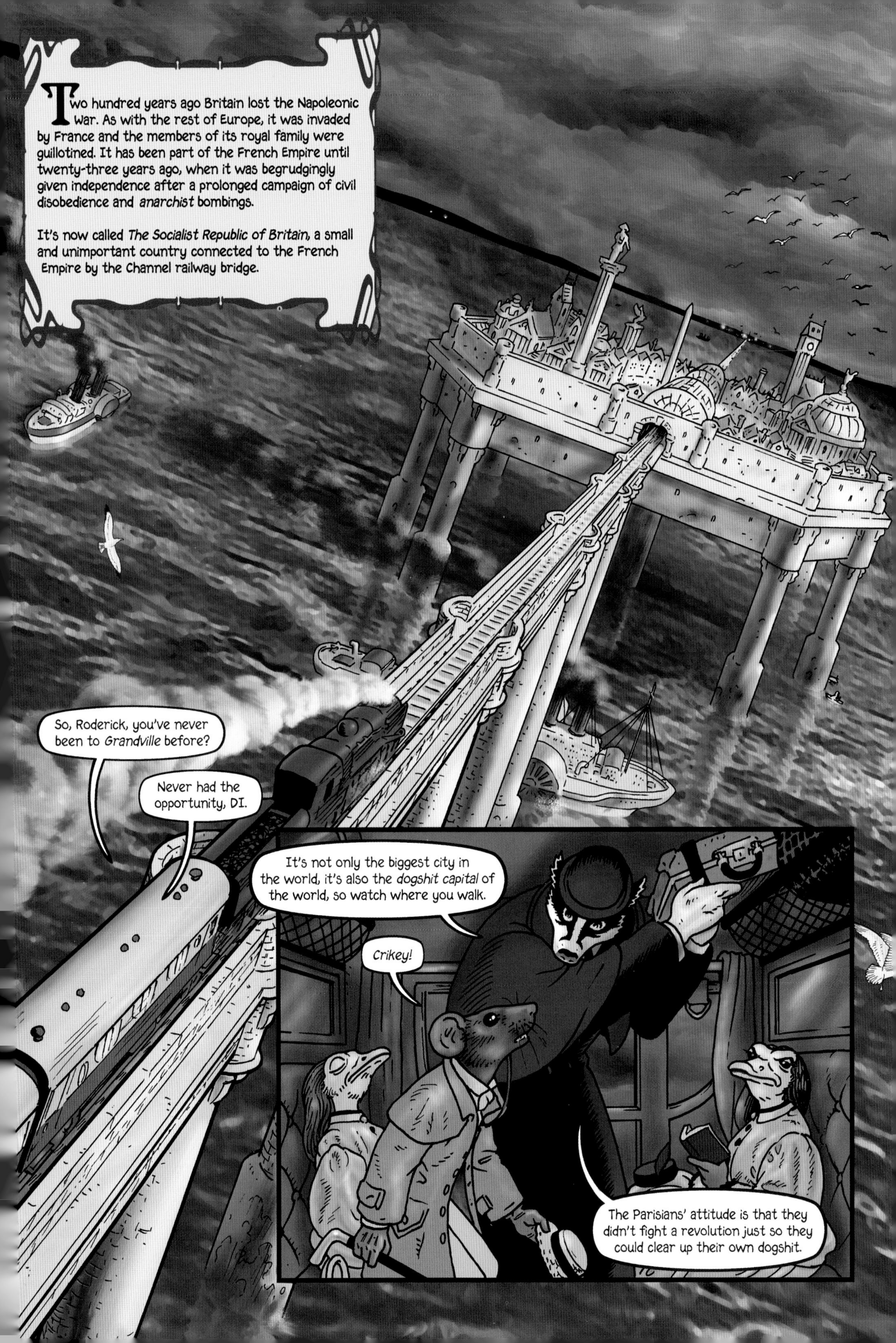
Two hundred years ago Britain lost the Napoleonic War. As with the rest of Europe, it was invaded by France and the members of its royal family were guillotined. It has been part of the French Empire until twenty-three years ago, when it was begrudgingly given independence after a prolonged campaign of civil disobedience and *anarchist* bombings.
It's now called *The Socialist Republic of Britain*, a small and unimportant country connected to the French Empire by the Channel railway bridge.
So, Roderick, you've never been to *Grandville* before?
Never had the opportunity, DI.
It's not only the biggest city in the world, it's also the *dogshit capital* of the world, so watch where you walk.
Crikey!
The Parisians' attitude is that they didn't fight a revolution just so they could clear up their own dogshit.

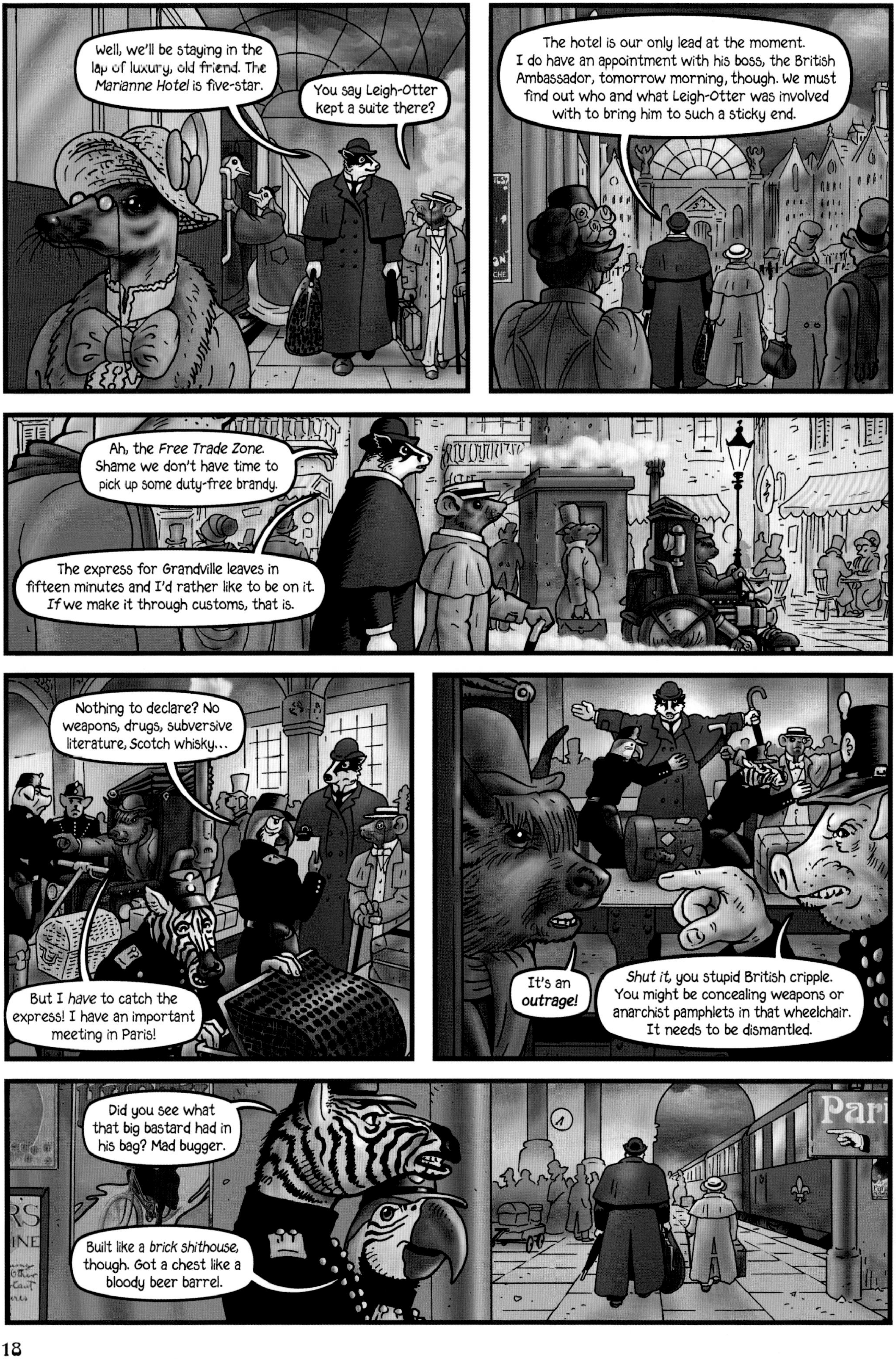
Well, we'll be staying in the lap of luxury, old friend. The *Marianne Hotel* is five-star.
You say Leigh-Otter kept a suite there?
The hotel is our only lead at the moment. I do have an appointment with his boss, the British Ambassador, tomorrow morning, though. We must find out who and what Leigh-Otter was involved with to bring him to such a sticky end.
Ah, the *Free Trade Zone*. Shame we don't have time to pick up some duty-free brandy.
The express for Grandville leaves in fifteen minutes and I'd rather like to be on it. *If* we make it through customs, that is.
Nothing to declare? No weapons, drugs, subversive literature, Scotch whisky...
But I *have* to catch the express! I have an important meeting in Paris!
It's an ***outrage!***
Shut it, you stupid British cripple. You might be concealing weapons or anarchist pamphlets in that wheelchair. It needs to be dismantled.
Did you see what that big bastard had in his bag? Mad bugger.
Built like a *brick shithouse*, though. Got a chest like a bloody beer barrel.
Pari

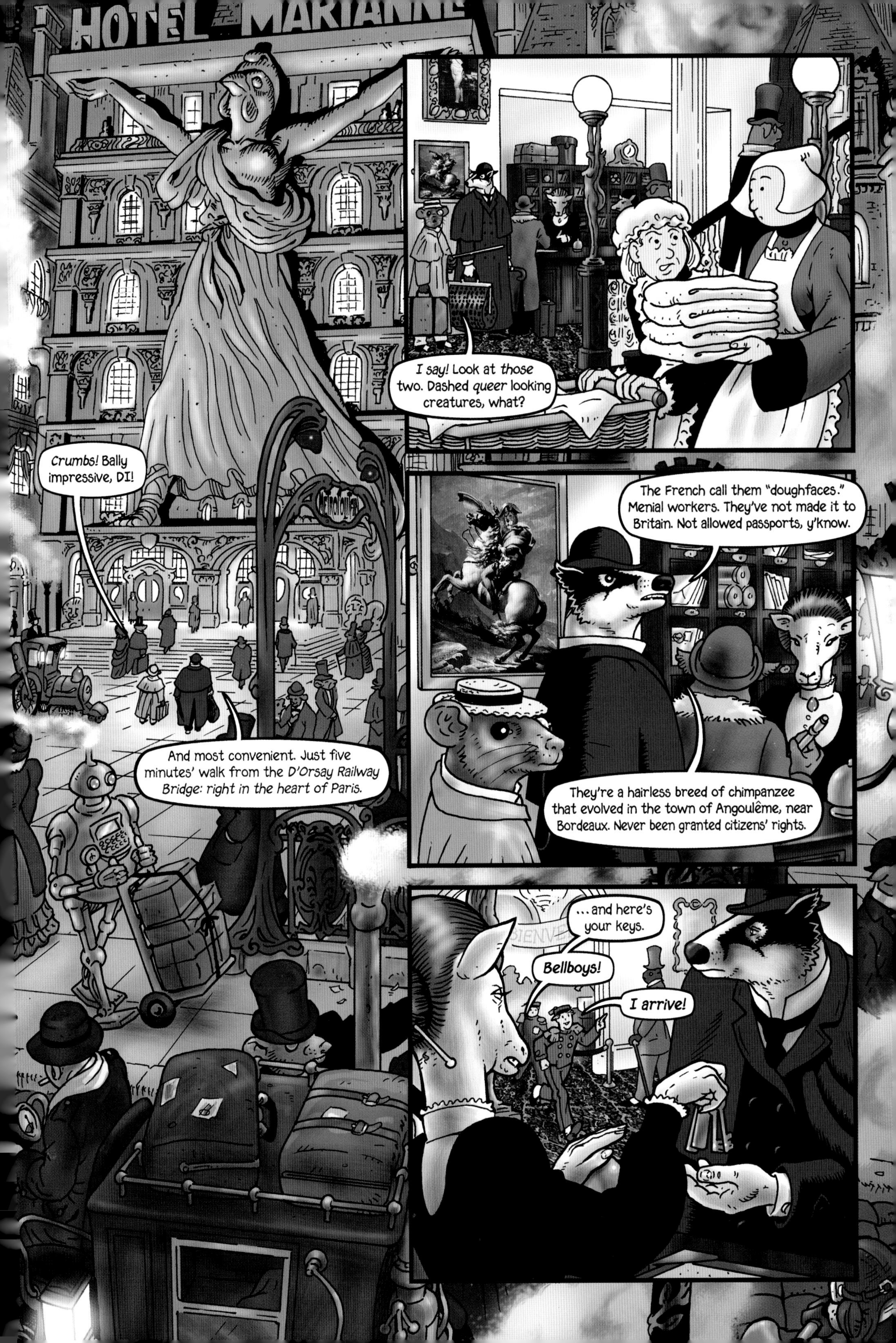
HOTEL MARIANNE
I say! Look at those two. Dashed queer looking creatures, what?
Crumbs! Bally impressive, DI!
METROPOLITAIN
And most convenient. Just five minutes' walk from the D'Orsay Railway Bridge: right in the heart of Paris.
The French call them "doughfaces." Menial workers. They've not made it to Britain. Not allowed passports, y'know.
They're a hairless breed of chimpanzee that evolved in the town of Angoulême, near Bordeaux. Never been granted citizens' rights.
...and here's your keys.
Bellboys!
I arrive!

Let me take that, sir!

If you insist.

Sure you don't want some help?

N-no, sir! I'd lose my job. They'll replace me with an automaton!

Roderick. Go ahead. I'll be a while.

See you in the lobby in twenty minutes.

Right-o.

Hello. What's going on here?

Arms dealers' convention, sir. Here all week. See the lady over there?

Madame Krupp, that is. She's famous. And rich. Biggest arms manufacturer here. She owns the newspapers too.

ACCÈS INTERDIT AU PUBLIC

I know who she *is*, lad.

Hmm. Look at that.

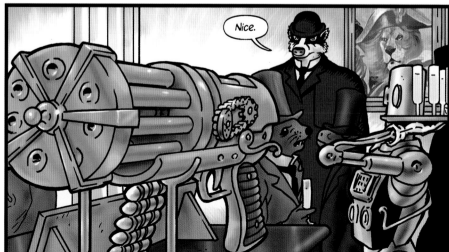

Nice.

20

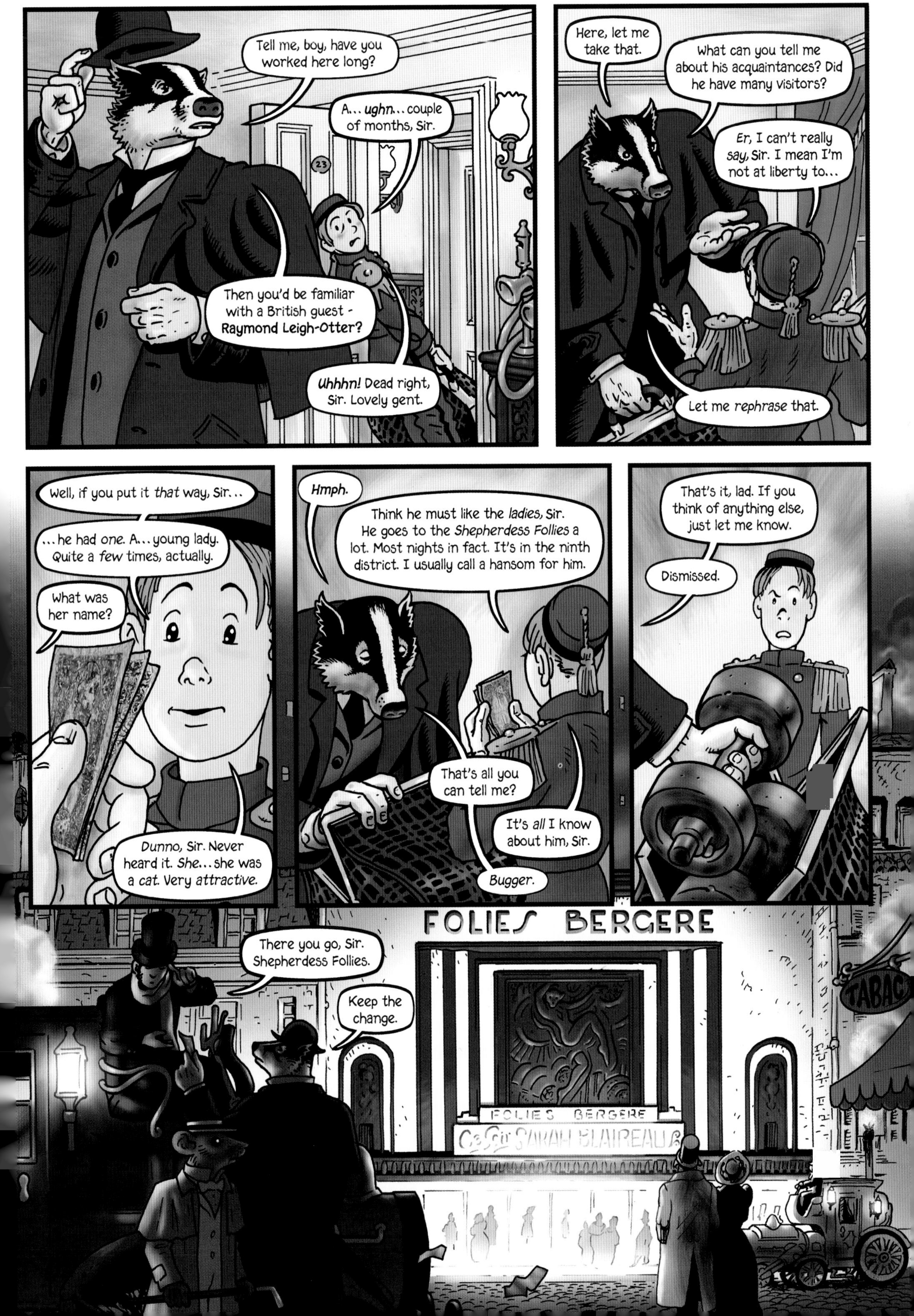
Tell me, boy, have you worked here long?
A... *ughn*... couple of months, Sir.
Then you'd be familiar with a British guest - **Raymond Leigh-Otter?**
Uhhhn! Dead right, Sir. Lovely gent.
Here, let me take that.
What can you tell me about his acquaintances? Did he have many visitors?
Er, I can't really *say*, Sir. I mean I'm not at liberty to...
Let me *rephrase* that.
Well, if you put it *that* way, Sir...
...he had *one*. A... young lady. Quite a *few* times, actually.
What was her name?
Dunno, Sir. Never heard it. *She*... she was a *cat*. Very *attractive*.
Hmph.
Think he must like the *ladies*, Sir. He goes to the *Shepherdess Follies* a lot. Most nights in fact. It's in the ninth district. I usually call a hansom for him.
That's all you can tell me?
It's *all* I know about him, Sir.
Bugger.
That's it, lad. If you think of anything else, just let me know.
Dismissed.
FOLIES BERGERE
There you go, Sir. Shepherdess Follies.
Keep the change.
FOLIES BERGERE
SARAH BLAIREAU
TABAC

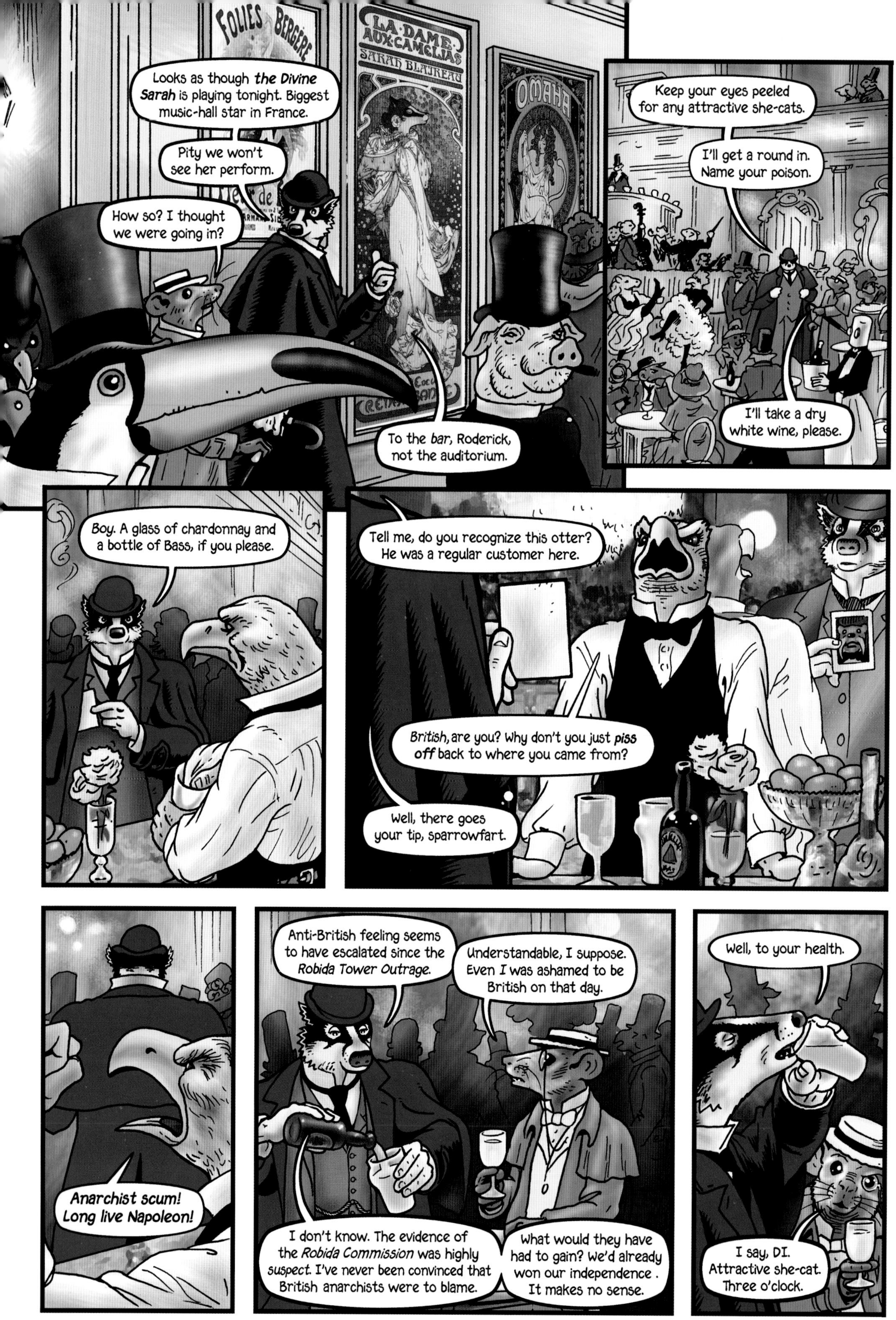
FOLIES BERGÈRE
LA DAME AUX CAMELIAS
SARAH BLAJREAU
OMAHA
Looks as though *the Divine Sarah* is playing tonight. Biggest music-hall star in France.
Pity we won't see her perform.
How so? I thought we were going in?
To the *bar*, Roderick, not the auditorium.
Keep your eyes peeled for any attractive she-cats.
I'll get a round in. Name your poison.
I'll take a dry white wine, please.
Boy. A glass of chardonnay and a bottle of Bass, if you please.
Tell me, do you recognize this otter? He was a regular customer here.
British, are you? Why don't you just *piss off* back to where you came from?
Well, there goes your tip, sparrowfart.
Anarchist scum! Long live Napoleon!
Anti-British feeling seems to have escalated since the *Robida Tower Outrage*.
Understandable, I suppose. Even *I* was ashamed to be British on that day.
I don't know. The evidence of the *Robida Commission* was highly *suspect*. I've never been convinced that British anarchists were to blame.
What would they have had to gain? We'd already won our independence . It makes no sense.
Well, to your health.
I say, DI. Attractive she-cat. Three o'clock.

"Mind if we join you?"

"Go away. Just leave me alone, you..."

"No. Get me a drink. Absinthe. A bottle."

"Certainly. Roderick?"

"LeBrock. My card."

"I couldn't help noticing that you're upset."

"A travelling salesman?"

"My companion and I are here for a short holiday. See the sights, you know? And you are?"

"Sabrina. I work here. Dancer."

"I...I..."

"huhh... uhuh... uhuh..."

"Come now, my dear, what's *wrong*?"

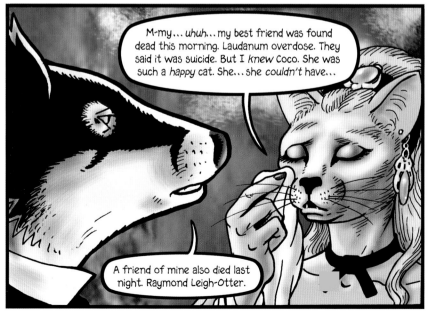

"M-my... *uhuh*... my best friend was found dead this morning. Laudanum overdose. They said it was suicide. But I *knew* Coco. She was such a *happy* cat. She... she *couldn't* have..."

"A friend of mine also died last night. Raymond Leigh-Otter."

"*What?* Raymond too? My God!"

"You knew him?"

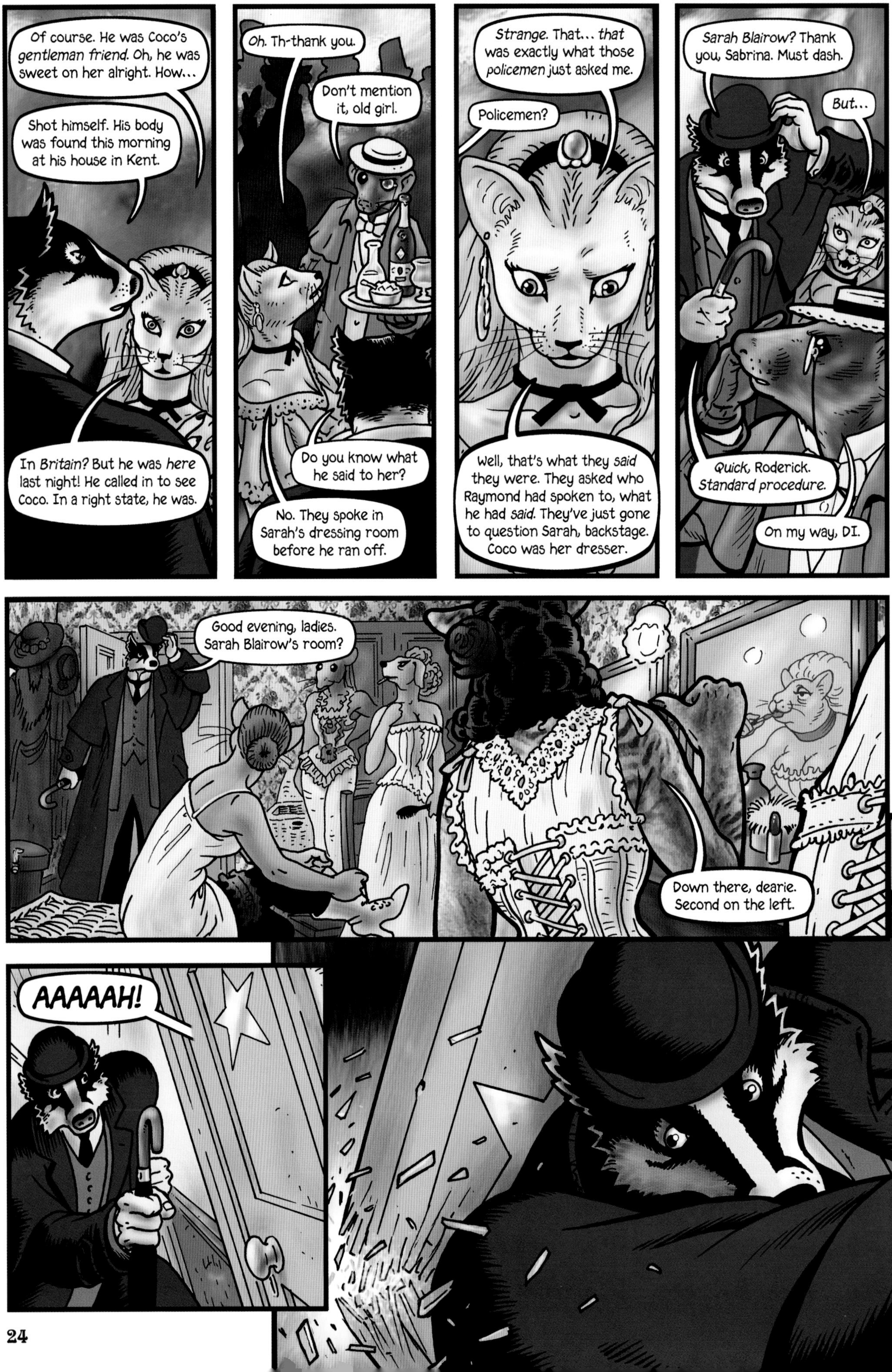
Of course. He was Coco's *gentleman friend*. Oh, he was sweet on her alright. How...
Shot himself. His body was found this morning at his house in Kent.
In *Britain*? But he was *here* last night! He called in to see Coco. In a right state, he was.
Oh. Th-thank you.
Don't mention it, old girl.
Do you know what he said to her?
No. They spoke in Sarah's dressing room before he ran off.
Strange. That... *that* was exactly what those *policemen* just asked me.
Policemen?
Well, that's what they *said* they were. They asked who Raymond had spoken to, what he had *said*. They've just gone to question Sarah, backstage. Coco was her dresser.
Sarah Blairow? Thank you, Sabrina. Must dash.
But...
Quick, Roderick. *Standard procedure*.
On my way, DI.
Good evening, ladies. Sarah Blairow's room?
Down there, dearie. Second on the left.
AAAAAH!

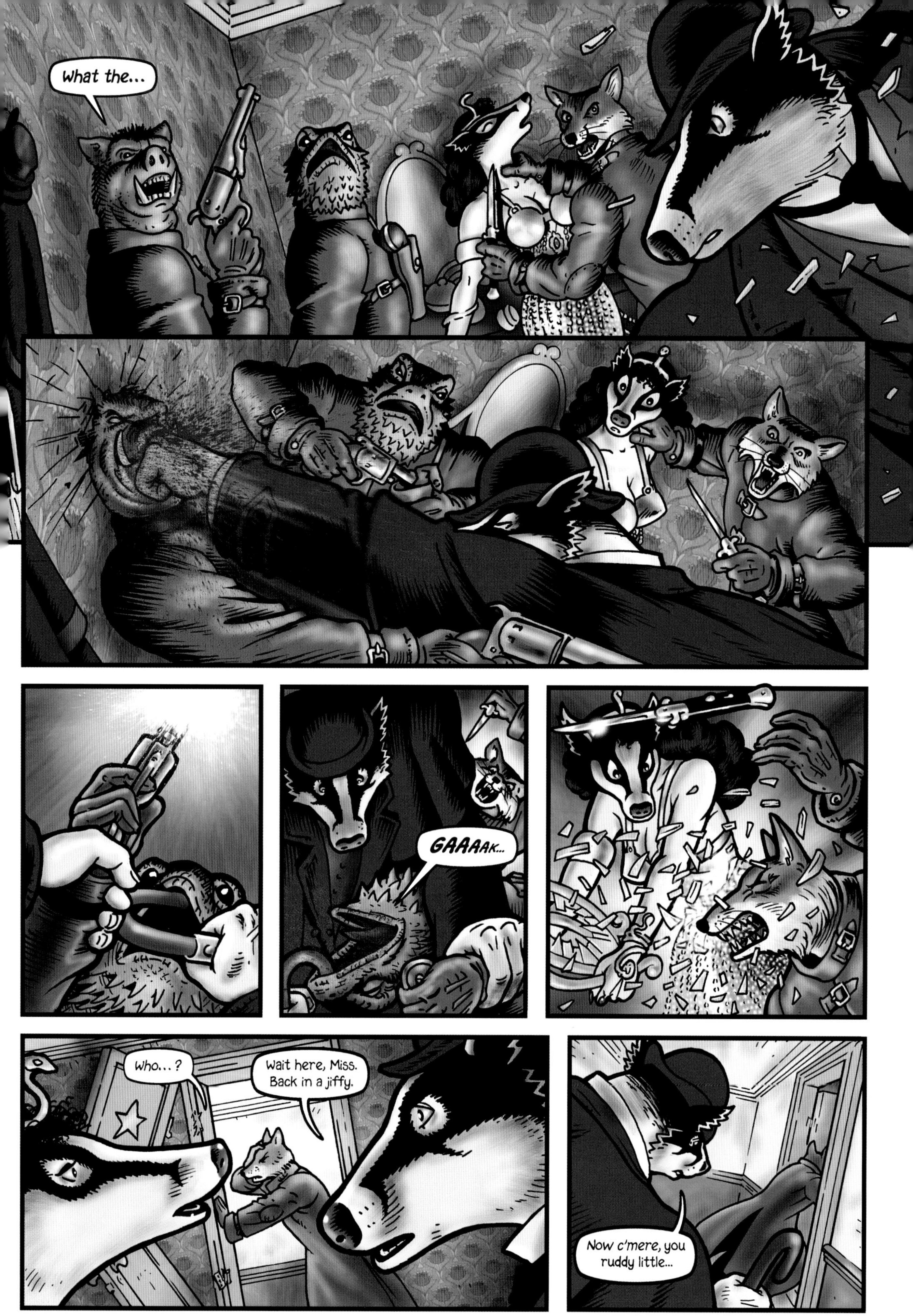
What the...
GAAAAK...
Who...?
Wait here, Miss. Back in a jiffy.
Now c'mere, you ruddy little...

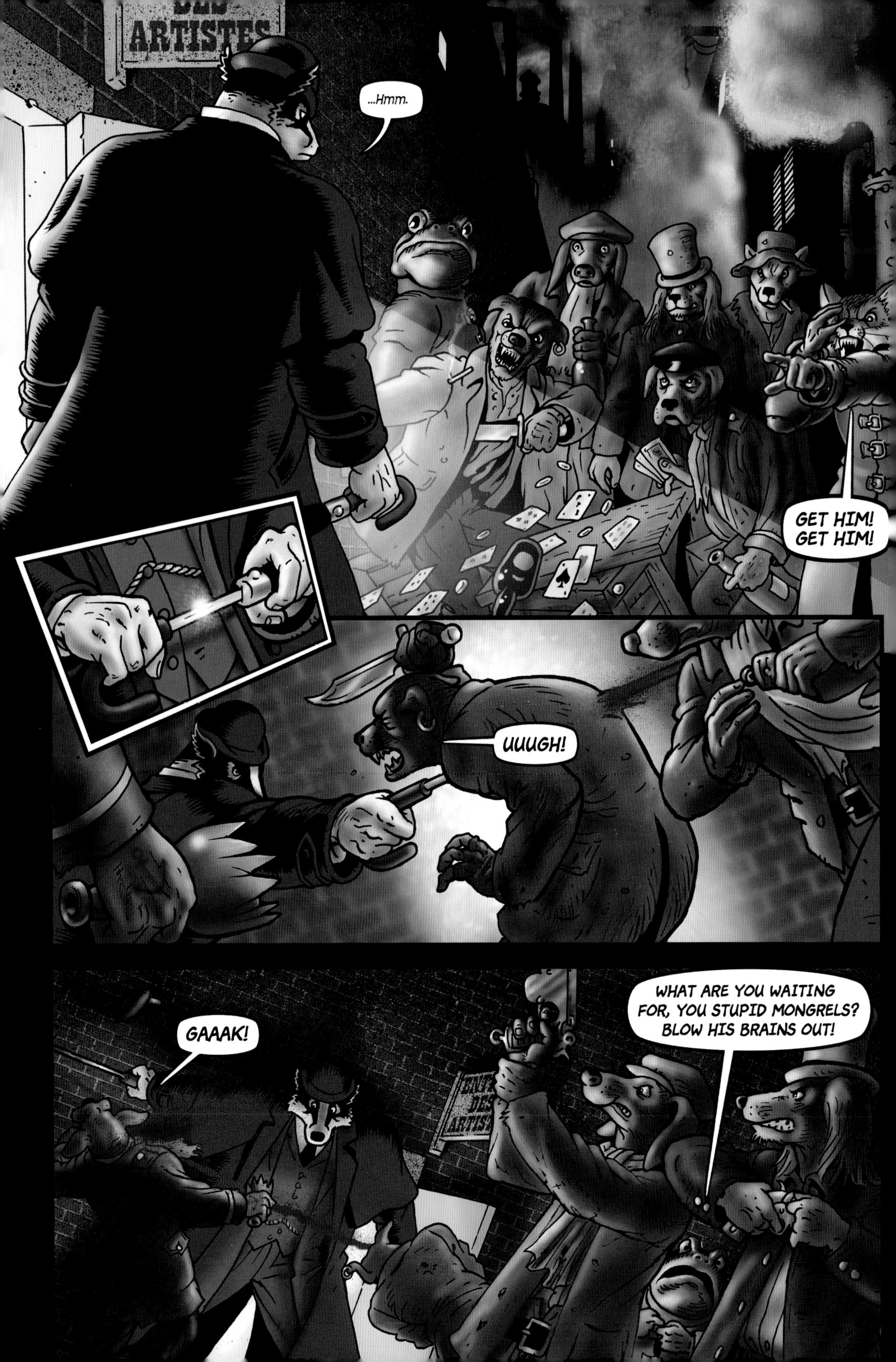

ARTISTES
...Hmm.
GET HIM! GET HIM!
UUUGH!
GAAAK!
WHAT ARE YOU WAITING FOR, YOU STUPID MONGRELS? BLOW HIS BRAINS OUT!

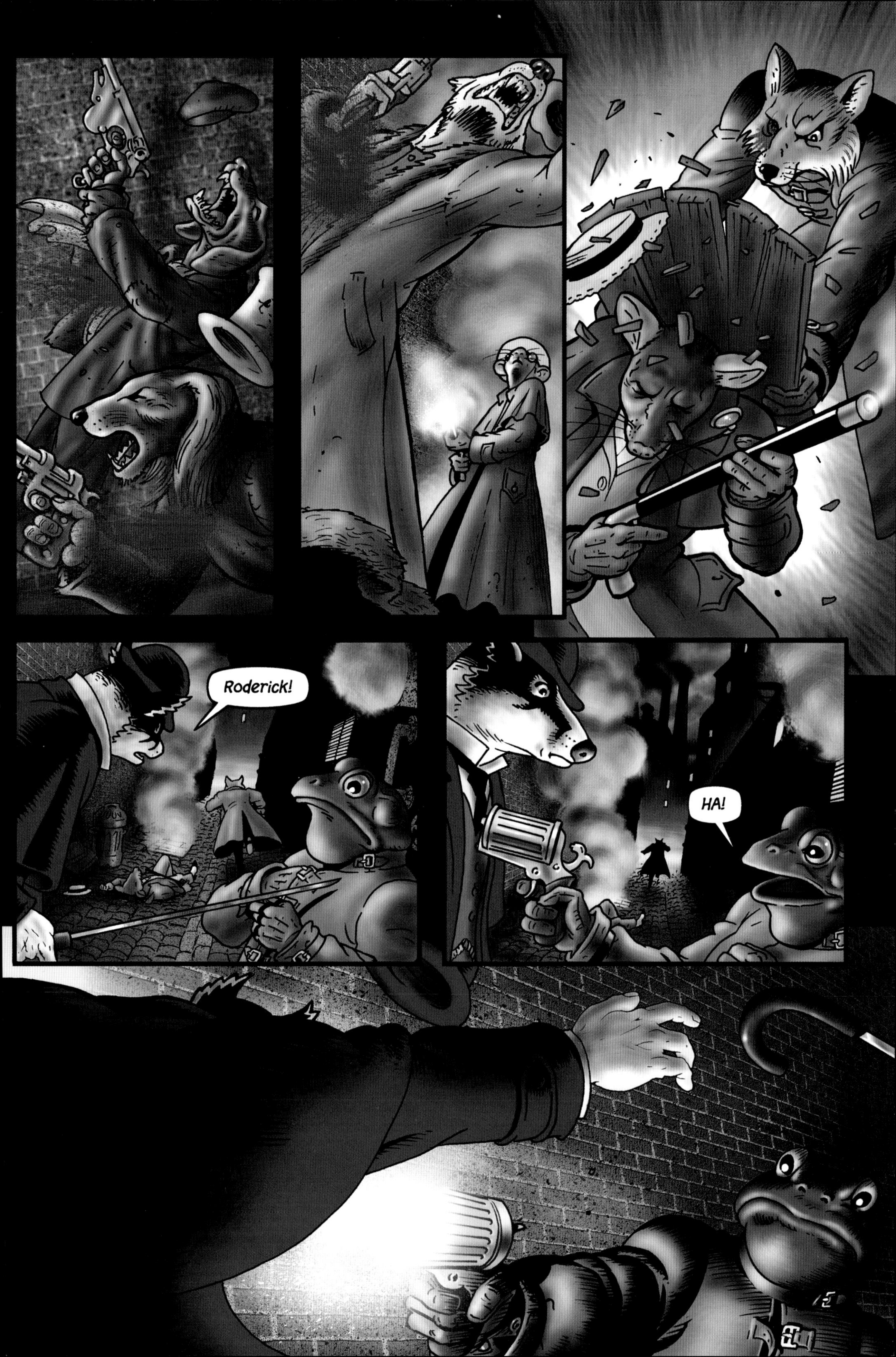
Roderick!
HA!

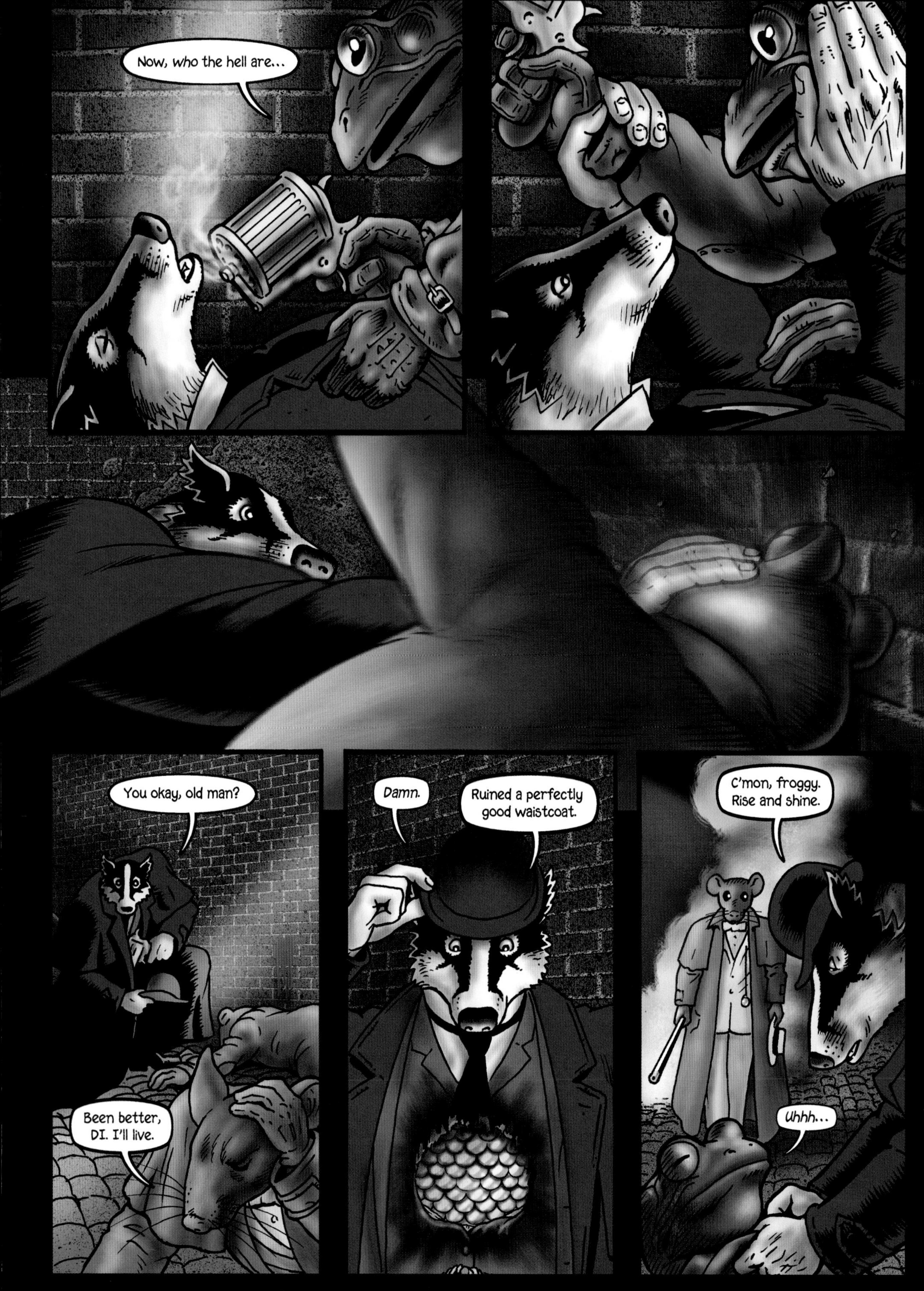
Now, who the hell are...
You okay, old man?
Been better, DI. I'll live.
Damn.
Ruined a perfectly good waistcoat.
C'mon, froggy. Rise and shine.
Uhhh...

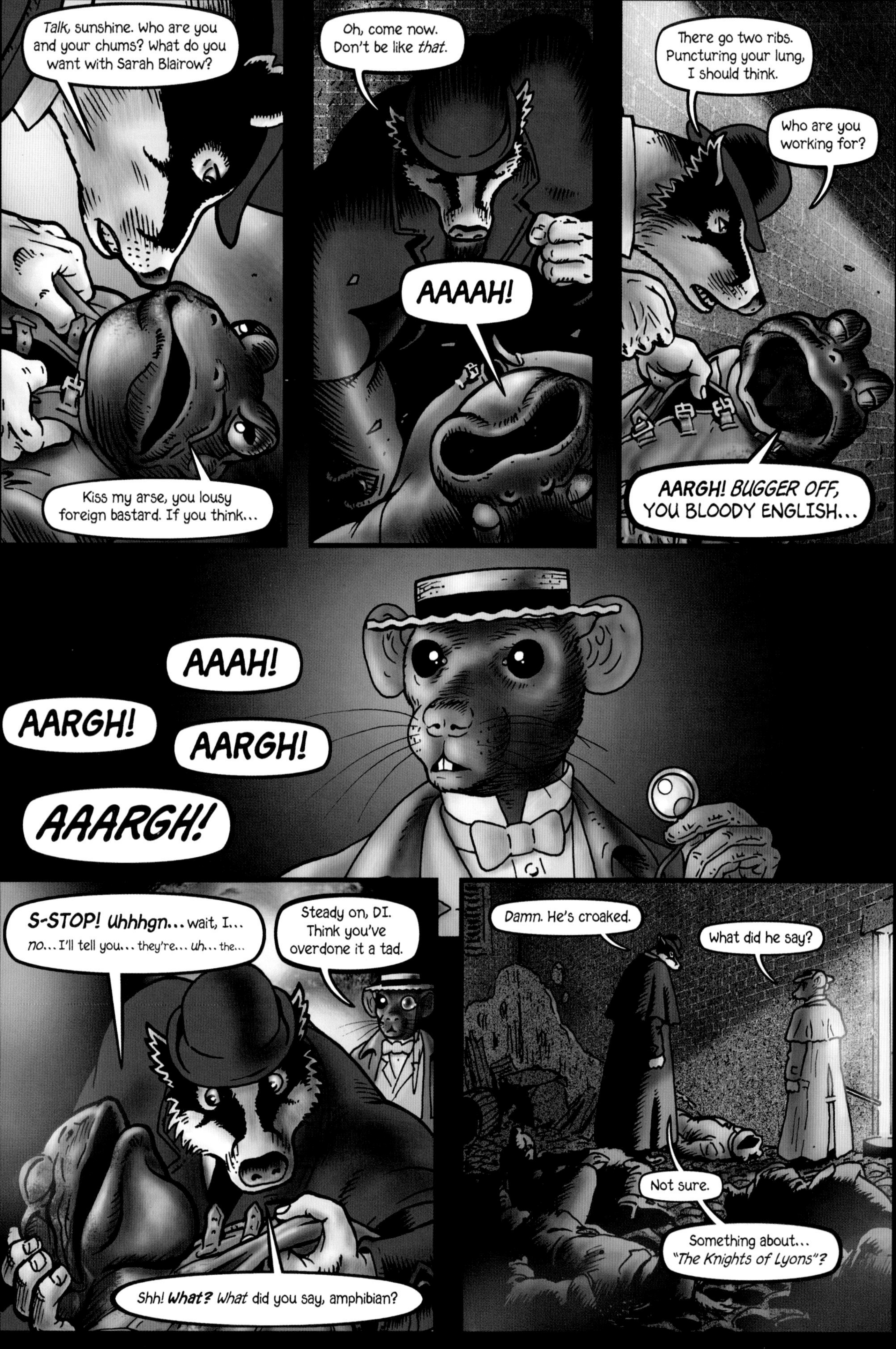
Talk, sunshine. Who are you and your chums? What do you want with Sarah Blairow?
Kiss my arse, you lousy foreign bastard. If you think...
Oh, come now. Don't be like *that.*
AAAAH!
There go two ribs. Puncturing your lung, I should think.
Who are you working for?
AARGH! *BUGGER OFF,* YOU BLOODY ENGLISH...
AAAH!
AARGH!
AARGH!
AAARGH!
S-STOP! Uhhhgn... wait, I... no... I'll tell you... they're... uh... the...
Steady on, DI. Think you've overdone it a tad.
Shh! **What?** *What* did you say, amphibian?
Damn. He's croaked.
What did he say?
Not sure.
Something about... *"The Knights of Lyons"?*

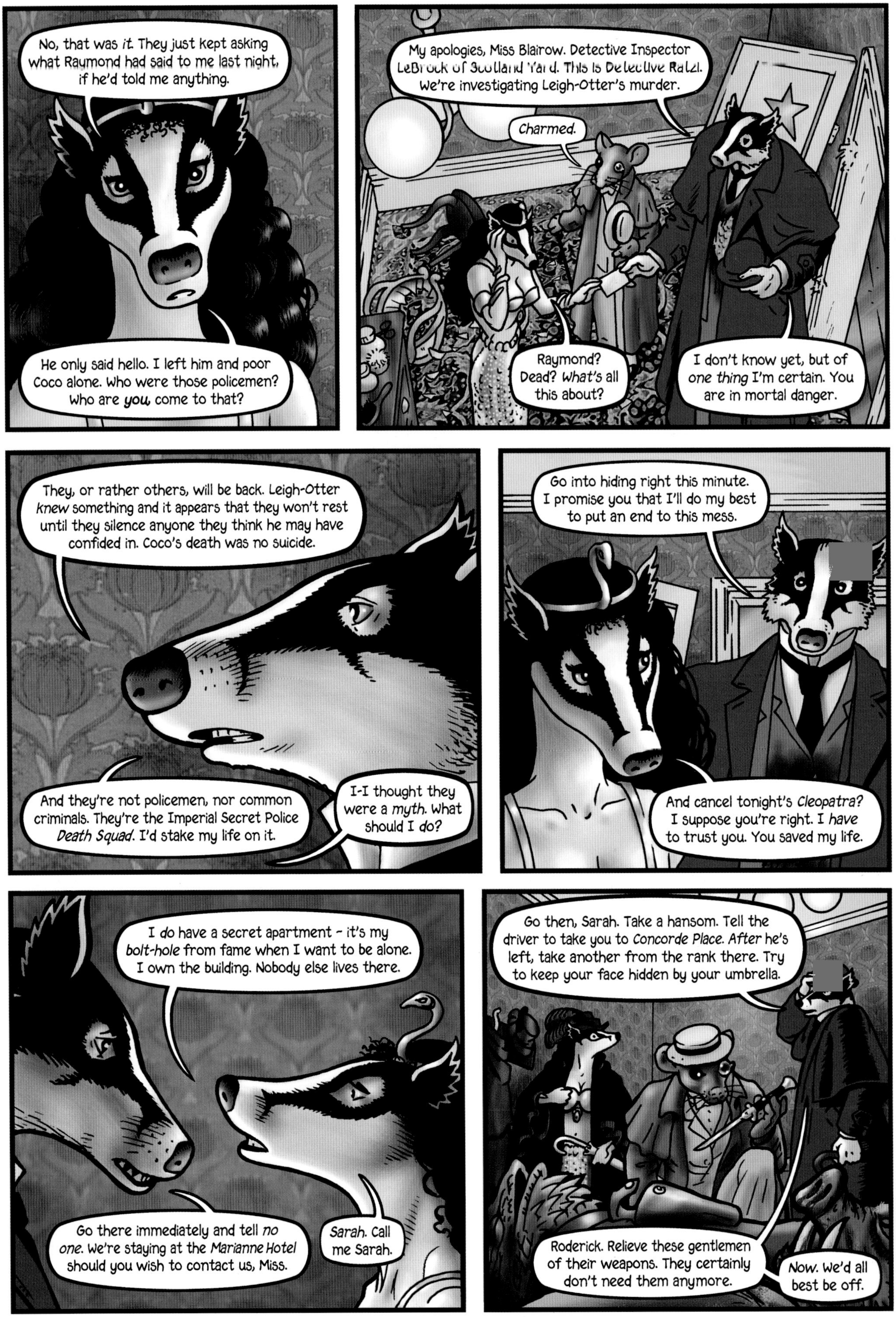
No, that was *it*. They just kept asking what Raymond had said to me last night, if he'd told me anything.
He only said hello. I left him and poor Coco alone. Who were those policemen? Who are **you**, come to that?
My apologies, Miss Blairow. Detective Inspector LeBrock of Scotland Yard. This is Detective Ratzi. We're investigating Leigh-Otter's murder.
Charmed.
Raymond? Dead? *What's* all this about?
I don't know yet, but of *one thing* I'm certain. You are in mortal danger.
They, or rather others, will be back. Leigh-Otter *knew* something and it appears that they won't rest until they silence anyone they think he may have confided in. Coco's death was no suicide.
And they're not policemen, nor common criminals. They're the Imperial Secret Police *Death Squad*. I'd stake my life on it.
I-I thought they were a *myth*. What should I *do?*
Go into hiding right this minute. I promise you that I'll do my best to put an end to this mess.
And cancel tonight's *Cleopatra?* I suppose you're right. I *have* to trust you. You saved my life.
I *do* have a secret apartment – it's my *bolt-hole* from fame when I want to be alone. I own the building. Nobody else lives there.
Go there immediately and tell *no one*. We're staying at the *Marianne Hotel* should you wish to contact us, Miss.
Sarah. Call me Sarah.
Go then, Sarah. Take a hansom. Tell the driver to take you to *Concorde Place*. *After* he's left, take another from the rank there. Try to keep your face hidden by your umbrella.
Roderick. Relieve these gentlemen of their weapons. They certainly don't need them anymore.
Now. We'd all best be off.

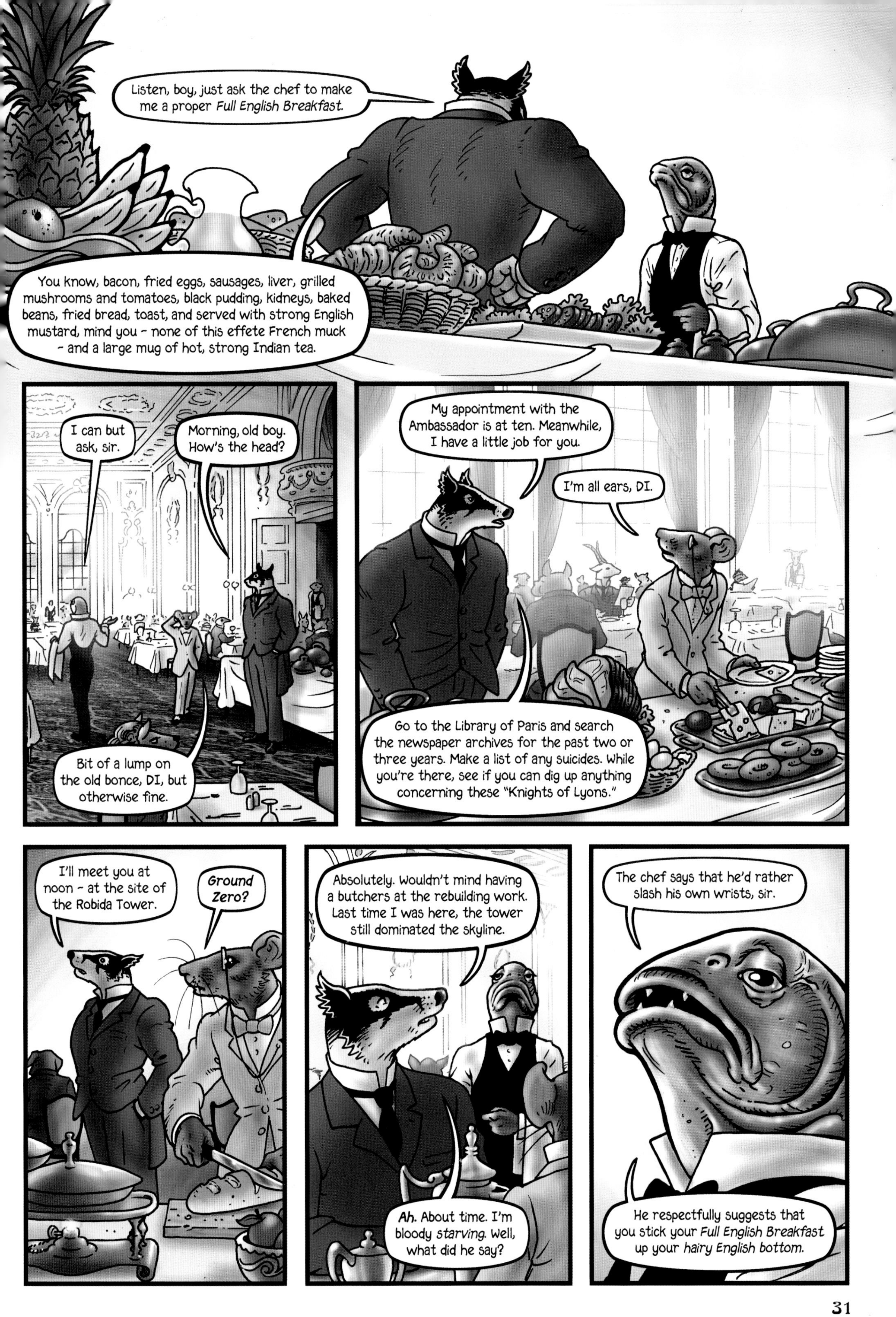
Listen, boy, just ask the chef to make me a proper *Full English Breakfast.*
You know, bacon, fried eggs, sausages, liver, grilled mushrooms and tomatoes, black pudding, kidneys, baked beans, fried bread, toast, and served with strong English mustard, mind you – none of this effete French muck – and a large mug of hot, strong Indian tea.
I can but ask, sir.
Morning, old boy. How's the head?
Bit of a lump on the old bonce, DI, but otherwise fine.
My appointment with the Ambassador is at ten. Meanwhile, I have a little job for you.
I'm all ears, DI.
Go to the Library of Paris and search the newspaper archives for the past two or three years. Make a list of any suicides. While you're there, see if you can dig up anything concerning these "Knights of Lyons."
I'll meet you at noon – at the site of the Robida Tower.
Ground Zero?
Absolutely. Wouldn't mind having a butchers at the rebuilding work. Last time I was here, the tower still dominated the skyline.
Ah. About time. I'm bloody *starving.* Well, what did he say?
The chef says that he'd rather slash his own wrists, sir.
He respectfully suggests that you stick your *Full English Breakfast* up your *hairy* English bottom.

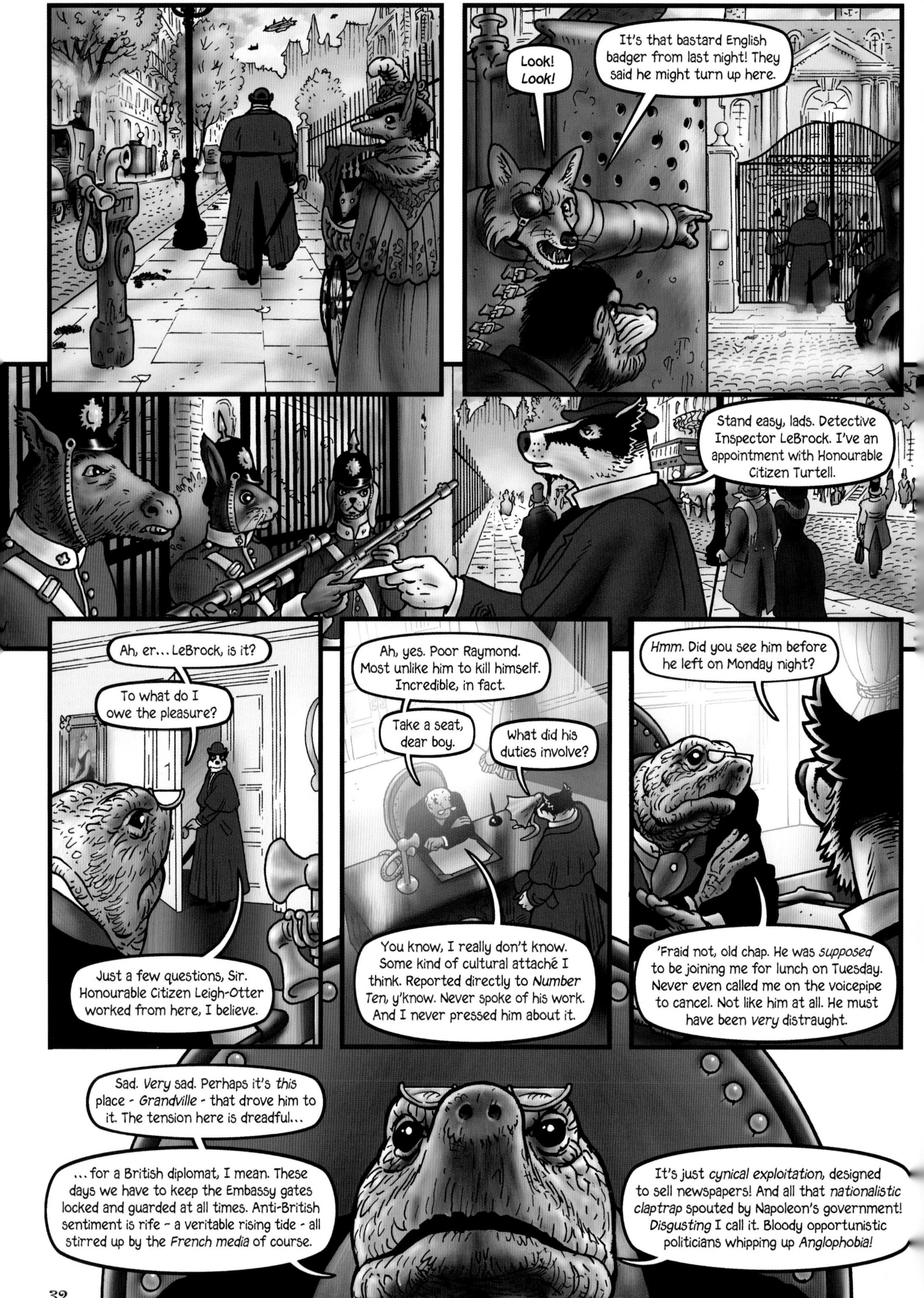
Look! Look!
It's that bastard English badger from last night! They said he might turn up here.
Stand easy, lads. Detective Inspector LeBrock. I've an appointment with Honourable Citizen Turtell.
Ah, er... LeBrock, is it?
To what do I owe the pleasure?
Just a few questions, Sir. Honourable Citizen Leigh-Otter worked from here, I believe.
Ah, yes. Poor Raymond. Most unlike him to kill himself. Incredible, in fact.
Take a seat, dear boy.
What did his duties involve?
You know, I really don't know. Some kind of cultural attaché I think. Reported directly to *Number Ten,* y'know. Never spoke of his work. And I never pressed him about it.
Hmm. Did you see him before he left on Monday night?
'Fraid not, old chap. He was *supposed* to be joining me for lunch on Tuesday. Never even called me on the voicepipe to cancel. Not like him at all. He must have been *very* distraught.
Sad. *Very* sad. Perhaps it's *this* place - *Grandville* - that drove him to it. The tension here is dreadful...
...for a British diplomat, I mean. These days we have to keep the Embassy gates locked and guarded at all times. Anti-British sentiment is rife - a veritable rising tide - all stirred up by the *French media* of course.
It's just *cynical exploitation,* designed to sell newspapers! And all that *nationalistic claptrap* spouted by Napoleon's government! *Disgusting* I call it. Bloody opportunistic politicians whipping up *Anglophobia!*

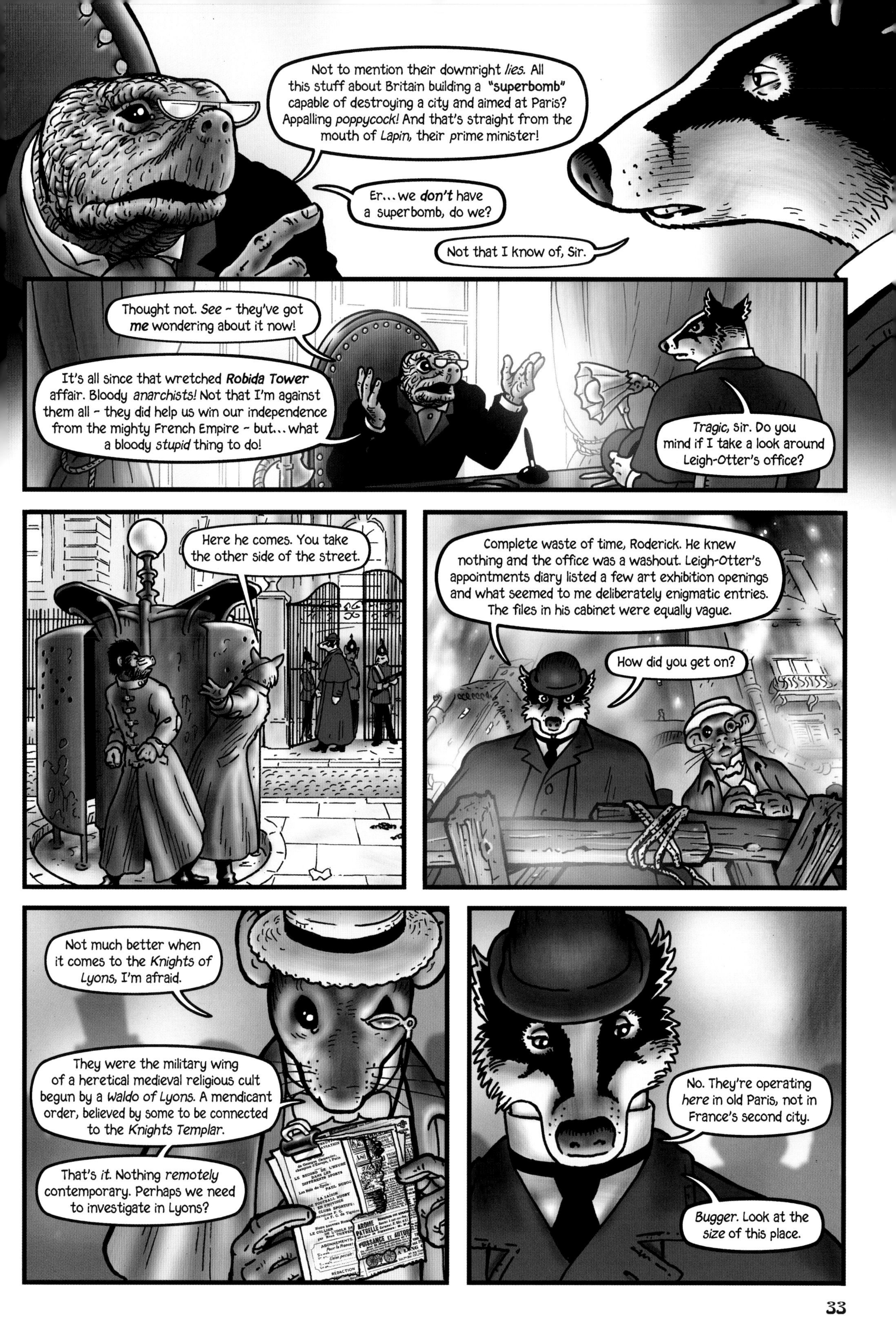
Not to mention their downright *lies.* All this stuff about Britain building a **"superbomb"** capable of destroying a city and aimed at Paris? Appalling *poppycock!* And that's straight from the mouth of *Lapin,* their *prime* minister!
Er... we ***don't*** have a superbomb, do we?
Not that I know of, Sir.
Thought not. *See* - they've got ***me*** wondering about it now!
It's all since that wretched **Robida Tower** affair. Bloody *anarchists!* Not that I'm against them all - they did help us win our independence from the mighty French Empire - but... what a bloody *stupid* thing to do!
Tragic, sir. Do you mind if I take a look around Leigh-Otter's office?
Here he comes. You take the other side of the street.
Complete waste of time, Roderick. He knew nothing and the office was a washout. Leigh-Otter's appointments diary listed a few art exhibition openings and what seemed to me deliberately enigmatic entries. The files in his cabinet were equally vague.
How did you get on?
Not much better when it comes to the *Knights of Lyons,* I'm afraid.
They were the military wing of a heretical medieval religious cult begun by a *Waldo of Lyons.* A mendicant order, believed by some to be connected to the *Knights Templar.*
That's *it.* Nothing *remotely* contemporary. Perhaps we need to investigate in Lyons?
No. They're operating *here* in old Paris, not in France's second city.
Bugger. Look at the *size* of this place.

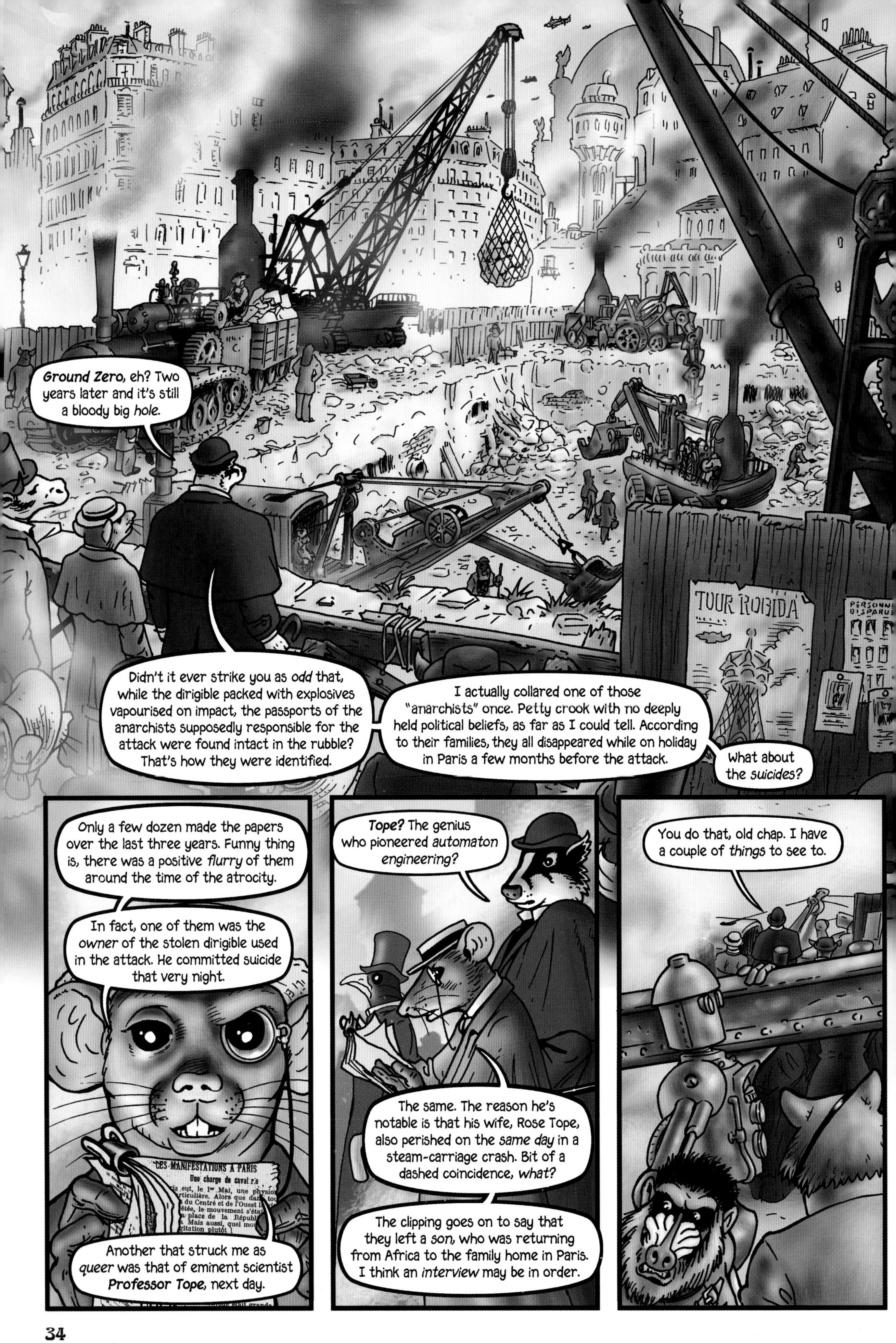

Ground Zero, eh? Two years later and it's still a bloody big hole.
Didn't it ever strike you as odd that, while the dirigible packed with explosives vapourised on impact, the passports of the anarchists supposedly responsible for the attack were found intact in the rubble? That's how they were identified.
I actually collared one of those "anarchists" once. Petty crook with no deeply held political beliefs, as far as I could tell. According to their families, they all disappeared while on holiday in Paris a few months before the attack.
What about the suicides?
TOUR ROBIDA
Only a few dozen made the papers over the last three years. Funny thing is, there was a positive flurry of them around the time of the atrocity.
In fact, one of them was the owner of the stolen dirigible used in the attack. He committed suicide that very night.
LES MANIFESTATIONS A PARIS
Another that struck me as queer was that of eminent scientist Professor Tope, next day.
Tope? The genius who pioneered automaton engineering?
The same. The reason he's notable is that his wife, Rose Tope, also perished on the same day in a steam-carriage crash. Bit of a dashed coincidence, what?
The clipping goes on to say that they left a son, who was returning from Africa to the family home in Paris. I think an interview may be in order.
You do that, old chap. I have a couple of things to see to.

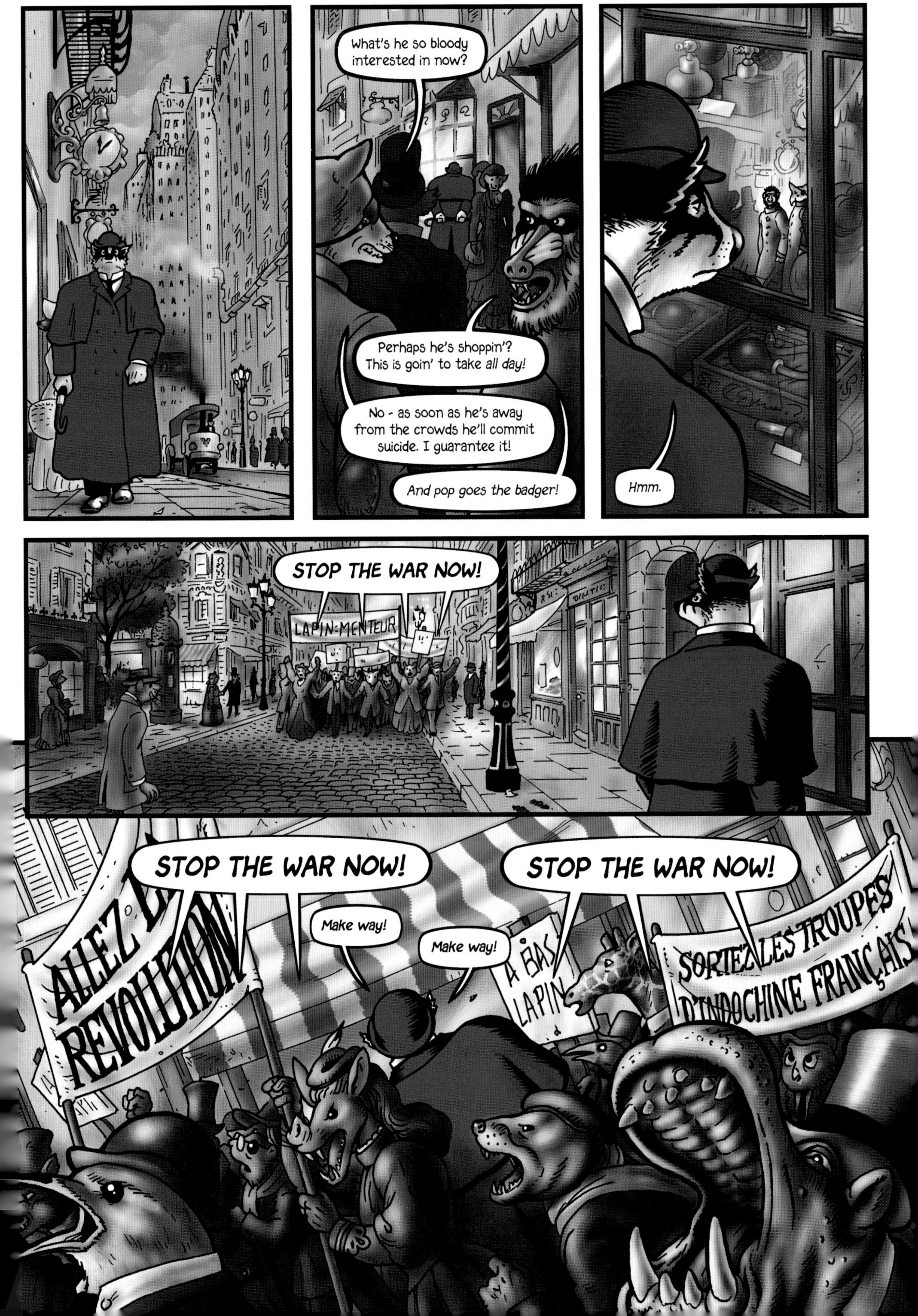
What's he so bloody interested in now?
Perhaps he's shoppin'? This is goin' to take *all day!*
No - as soon as he's away from the crowds he'll commit suicide. I guarantee it!
And pop goes the badger!
Hmm.
STOP THE WAR NOW!
LAPIN: MENTEUR
STOP THE WAR NOW!
STOP THE WAR NOW!
Make way!
Make way!
REVOLUTION
A BAS LAPIN
SORTEZ LES TROUPES D'INDOCHINE FRANÇAIS

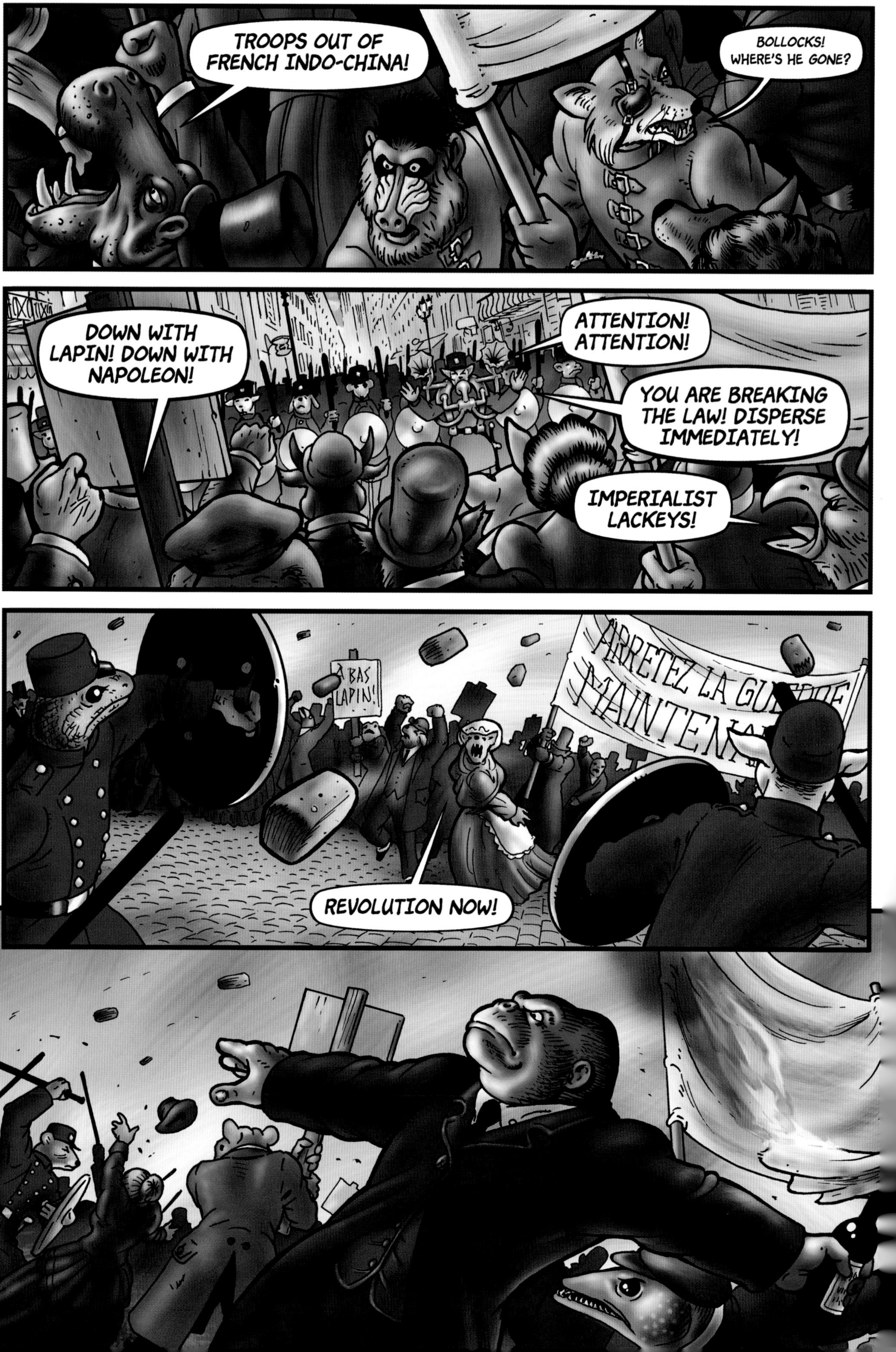
TROOPS OUT OF FRENCH INDO-CHINA!
BOLLOCKS! WHERE'S HE GONE?
DOWN WITH LAPIN! DOWN WITH NAPOLEON!
ATTENTION! ATTENTION!
YOU ARE BREAKING THE LAW! DISPERSE IMMEDIATELY!
IMPERIALIST LACKEYS!
À BAS LAPIN!
ARRETEZ LA
REVOLUTION NOW!

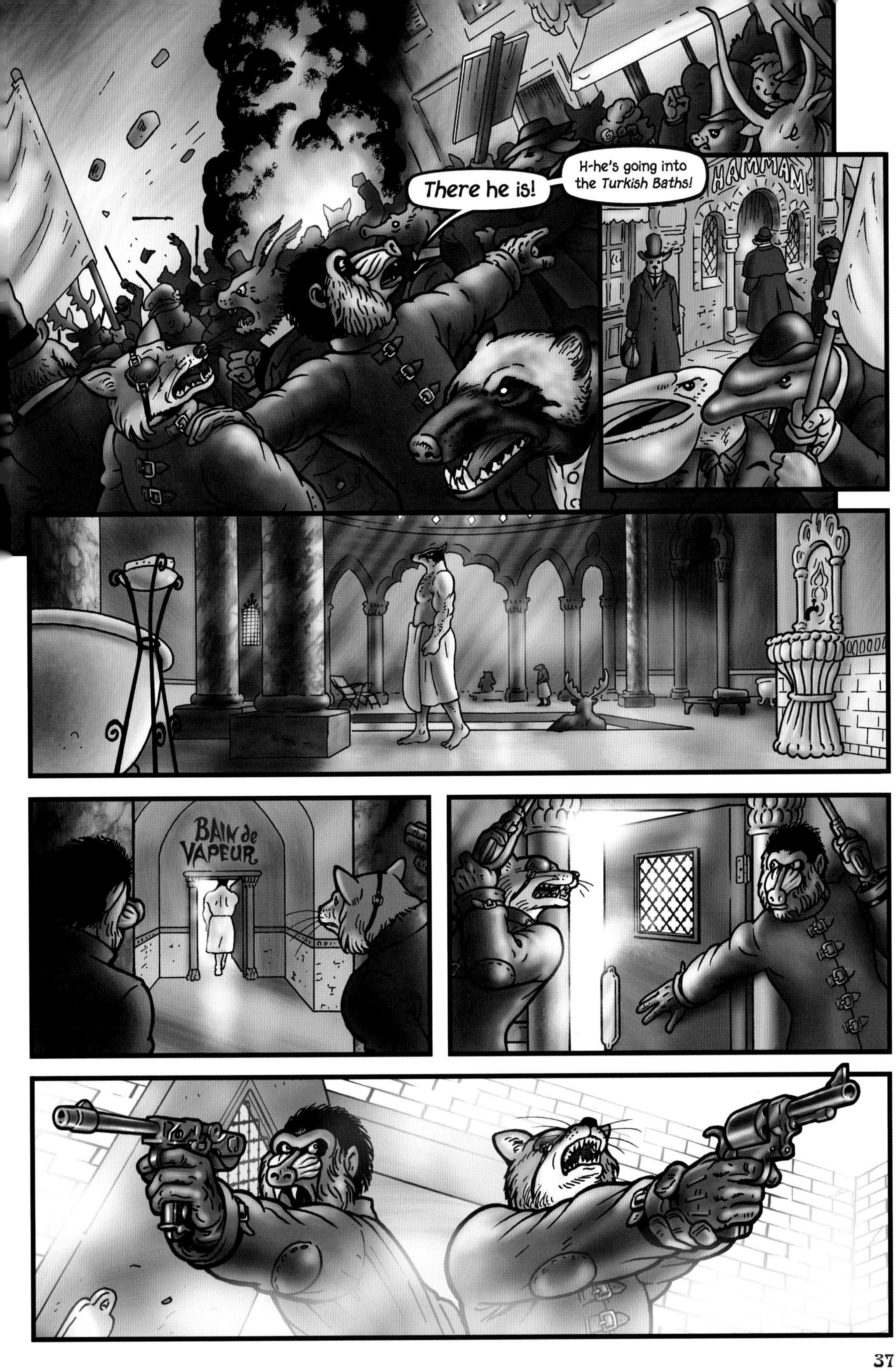

There he is!
H-he's going into the Turkish Baths!
HAMMAM
BAIN de VAPEUR

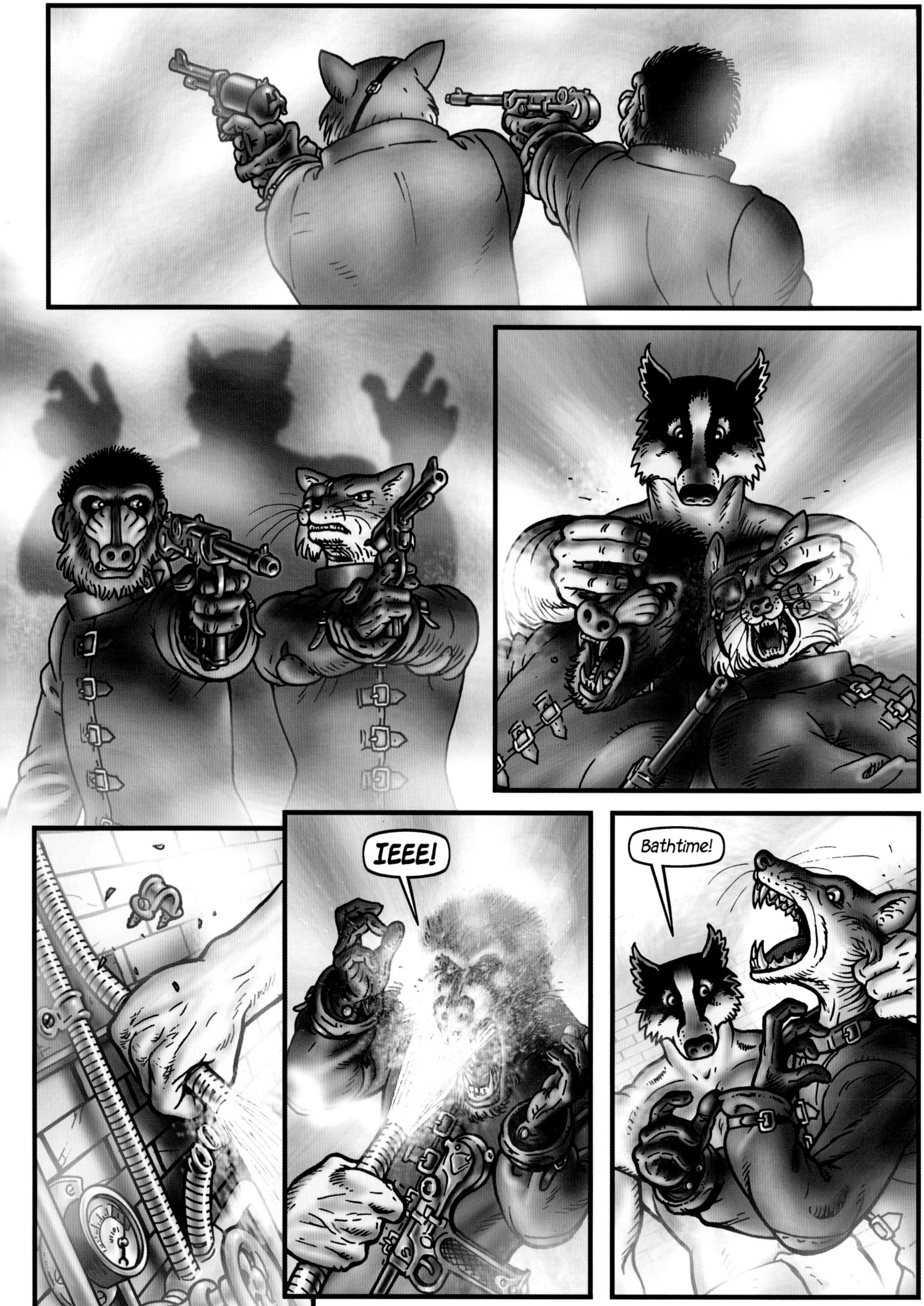
IEEE!
Bathtime!

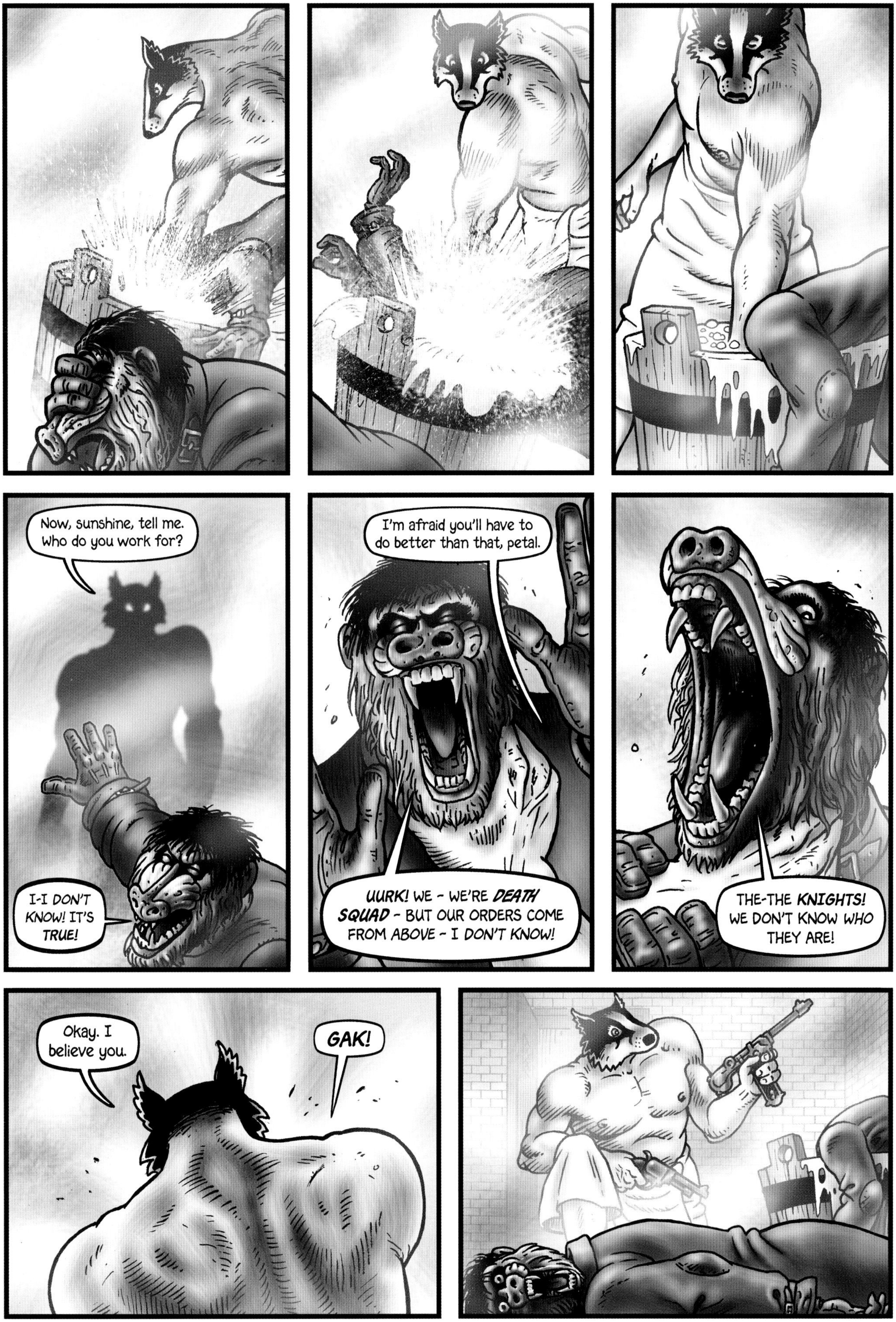

Now, sunshine, tell me. Who do you work for?
I-I DON'T KNOW! IT'S TRUE!
I'm afraid you'll have to do better than that, petal.
UURK! WE - WE'RE DEATH SQUAD - BUT OUR ORDERS COME FROM ABOVE - I DON'T KNOW!
THE-THE KNIGHTS! WE DON'T KNOW WHO THEY ARE!
Okay. I believe you.
GAK!

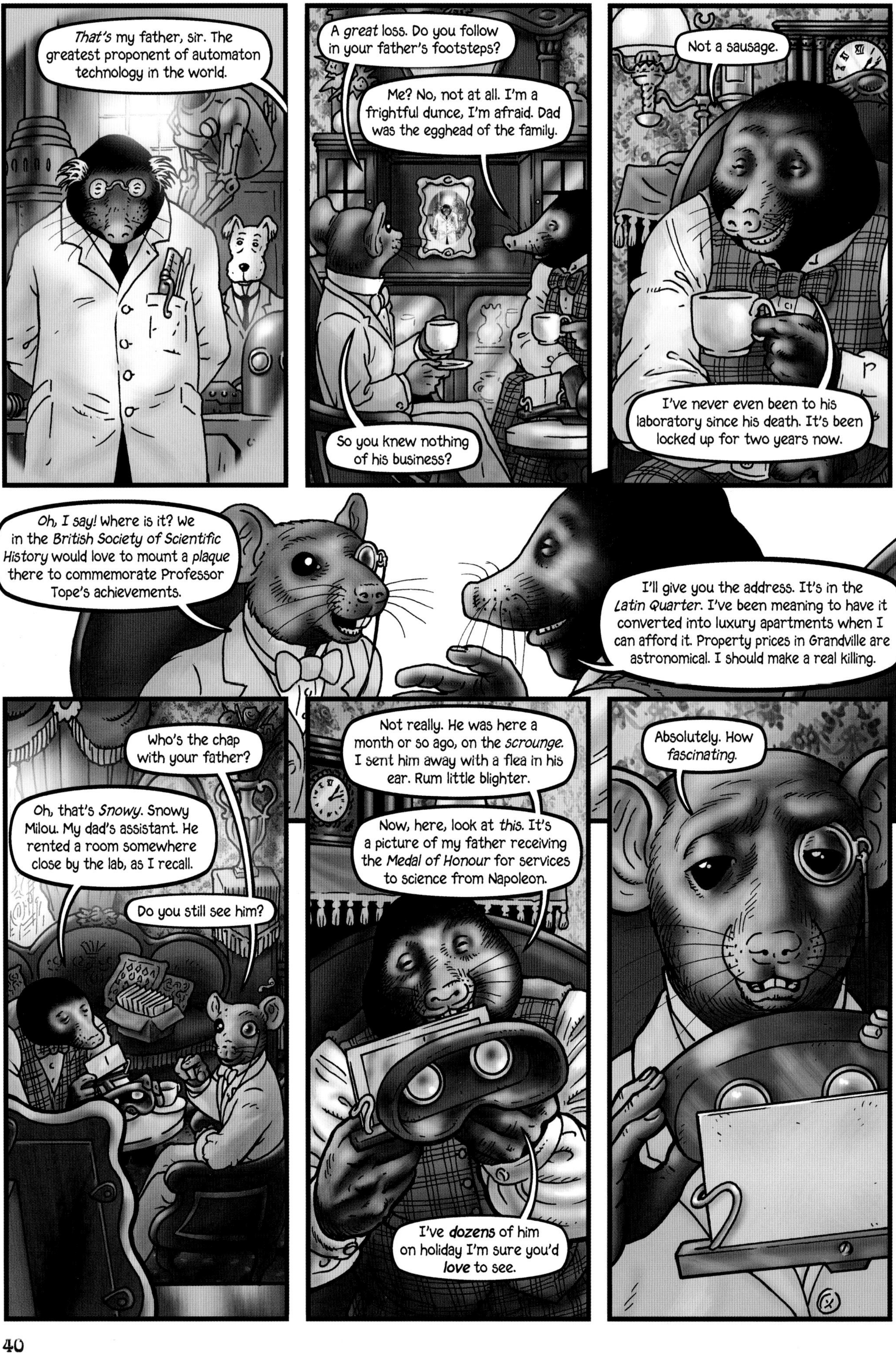

That's my father, sir. The greatest proponent of automaton technology in the world.
A *great* loss. Do you follow in your father's footsteps?
Me? No, not at all. I'm a frightful dunce, I'm afraid. Dad was the egghead of the family.
So you knew nothing of his business?
Not a sausage.
I've never even been to his laboratory since his death. It's been locked up for two years now.
Oh, I say! Where is it? We in the *British Society of Scientific History* would love to mount a *plaque* there to commemorate Professor Tope's achievements.
I'll give you the address. It's in the *Latin Quarter*. I've been meaning to have it converted into luxury apartments when I can afford it. Property prices in Grandville are astronomical. I should make a real killing.
Who's the chap with your father?
Oh, that's *Snowy*. Snowy Milou. My dad's assistant. He rented a room somewhere close by the lab, as I recall.
Do you still see him?
Not really. He was here a month or so ago, on the *scrounge*. I sent him away with a flea in his ear. Rum little blighter.
Now, here, look at *this*. It's a picture of my father receiving the *Medal of Honour* for services to science from Napoleon.
I've **dozens** of him on holiday I'm sure you'd **love** to see.
Absolutely. How *fascinating*.

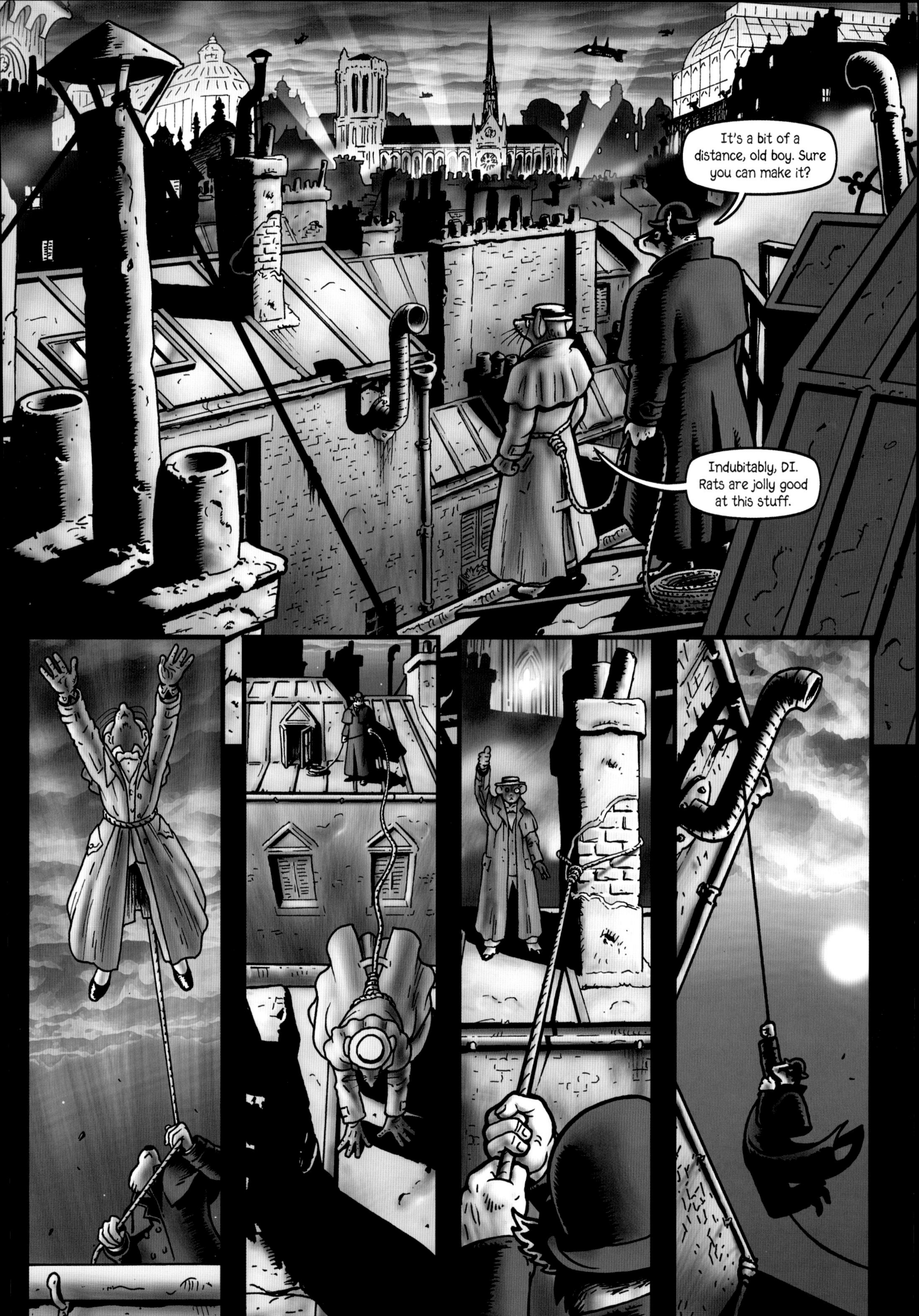
It's a bit of a distance, old boy. Sure you can make it?
Indubitably, DI. Rats are jolly good at this stuff.

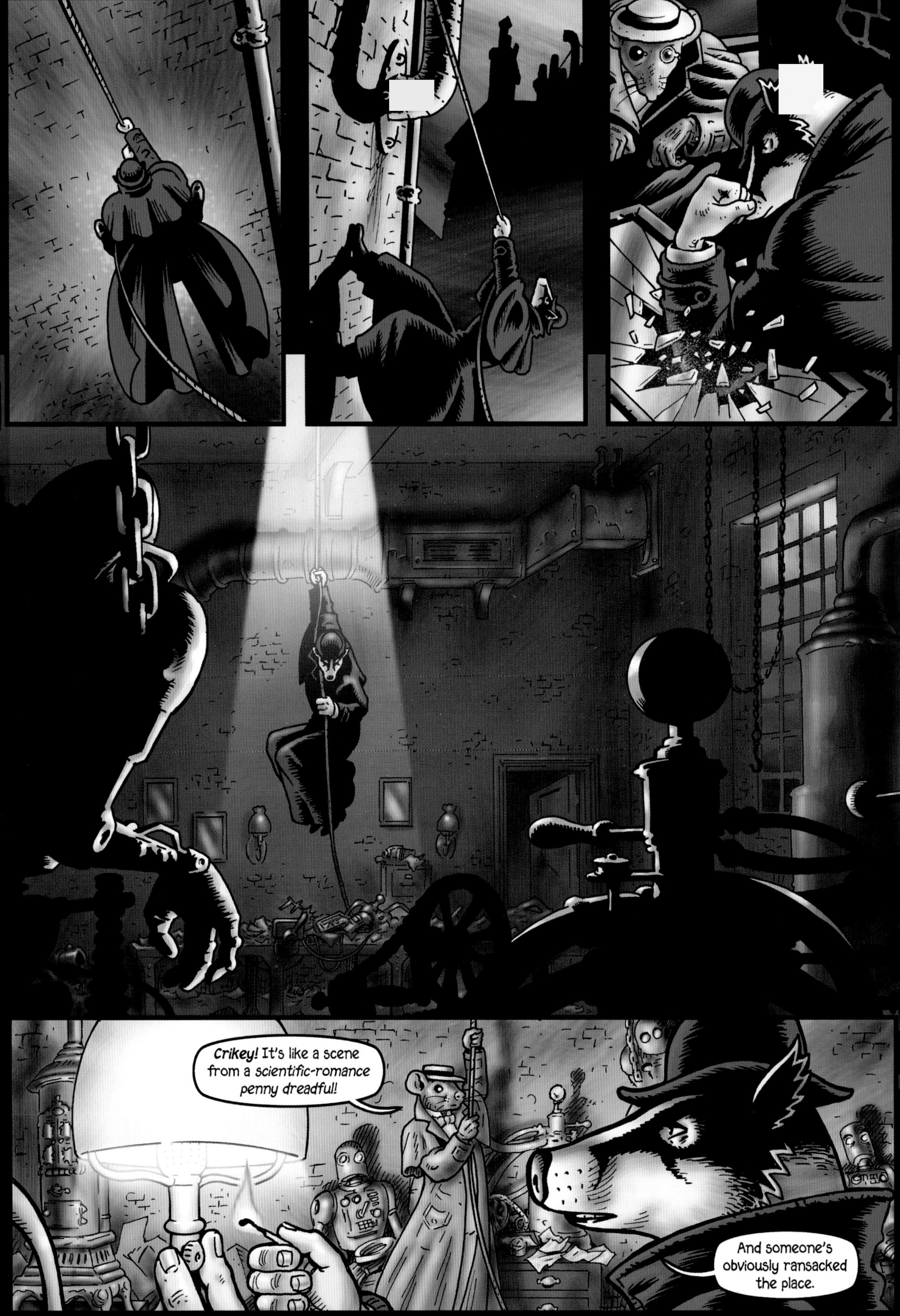
Crikey! It's like a scene from a *scientific-romance* penny *dreadful!*
And someone's obviously ransacked the place.

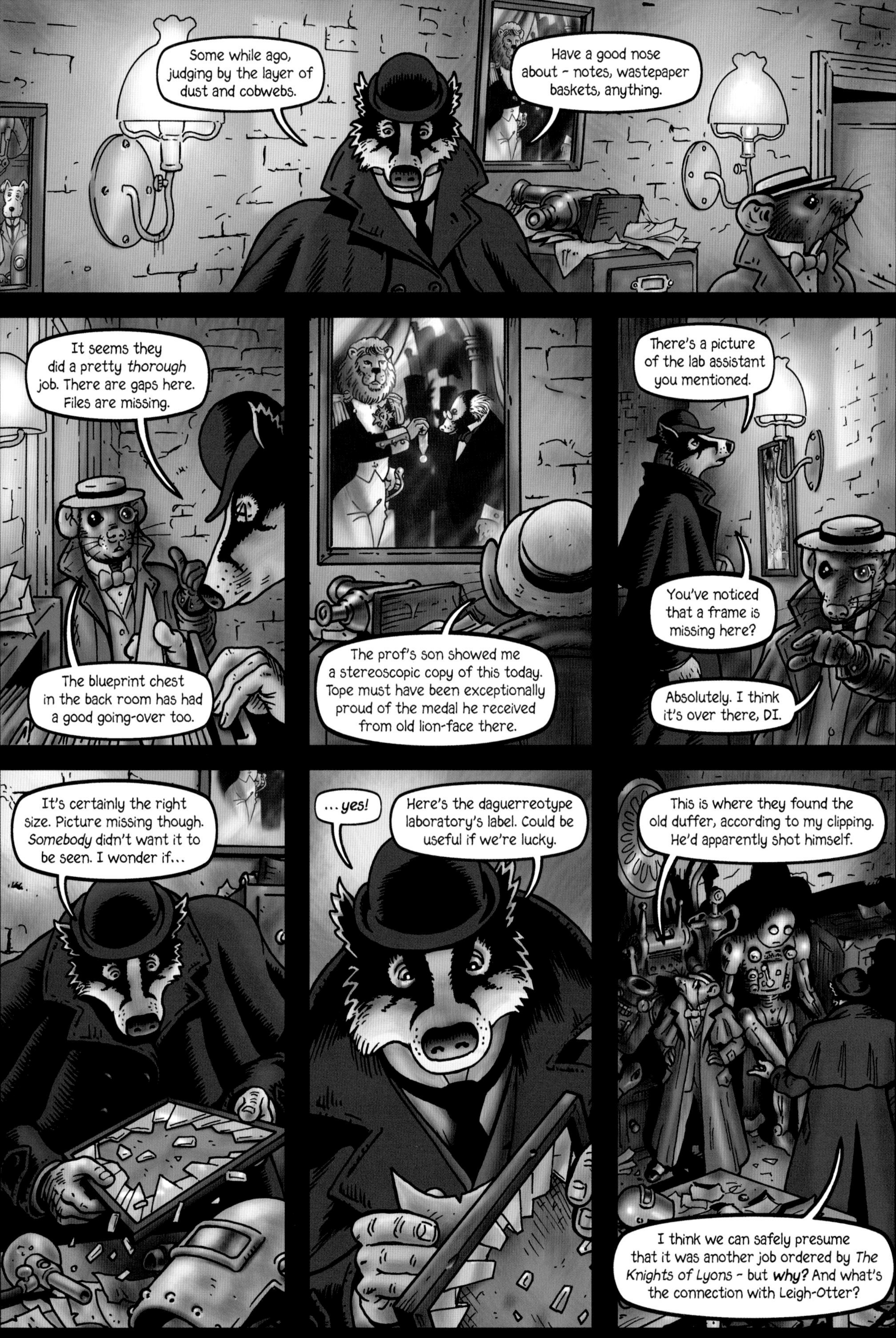
Some while ago, judging by the layer of dust and cobwebs.
Have a good nose about - notes, wastepaper baskets, anything.
It seems they did a pretty *thorough* job. There are gaps here. Files are missing.
The blueprint chest in the back room has had a good going-over too.
The prof's son showed me a stereoscopic copy of this today. Tope must have been exceptionally proud of the medal he received from old lion-face there.
There's a picture of the lab assistant you mentioned.
You've noticed that a frame is missing here?
Absolutely. I think it's over there, DI.
It's certainly the right size. Picture missing though. *Somebody* didn't want it to be seen. I wonder if...
...*yes!*
Here's the daguerreotype laboratory's label. Could be useful if we're lucky.
This is where they found the old duffer, according to my clipping. He'd apparently shot himself.
I think we can safely presume that it was another job ordered by *The Knights of Lyons* - but **why?** And what's the connection with Leigh-Otter?

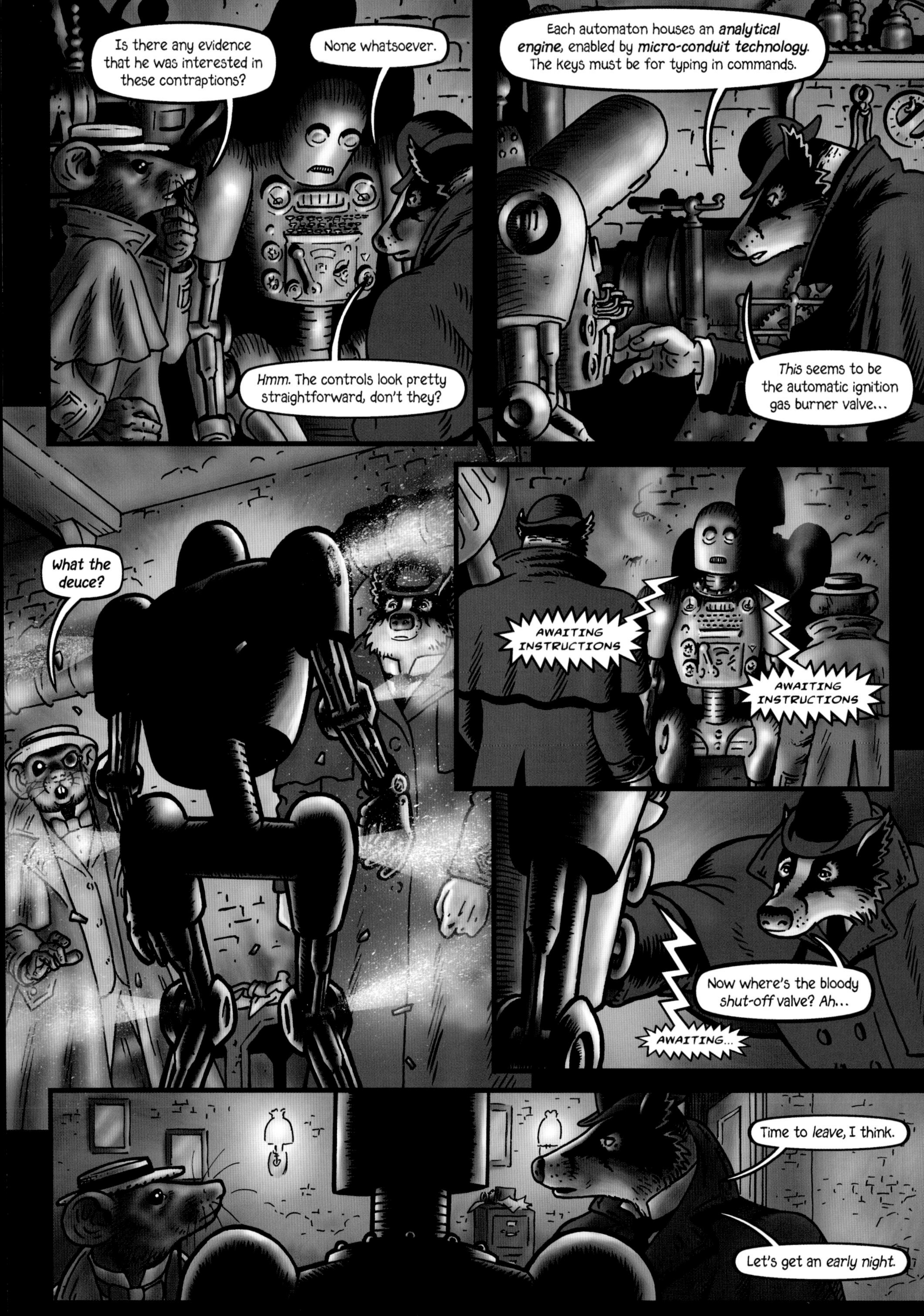
Is there any evidence that he was interested in these contraptions?
None whatsoever.
Hmm. The controls look pretty straightforward, don't they?
Each automaton houses an *analytical engine*, enabled by *micro-conduit technology*. The keys must be for typing in commands.
This seems to be the automatic ignition gas burner valve...
What the deuce?
AWAITING INSTRUCTIONS
AWAITING INSTRUCTIONS
Now where's the bloody *shut-off* valve? Ah...
AWAITING...
Time to *leave*, I think.
Let's get an *early night*.

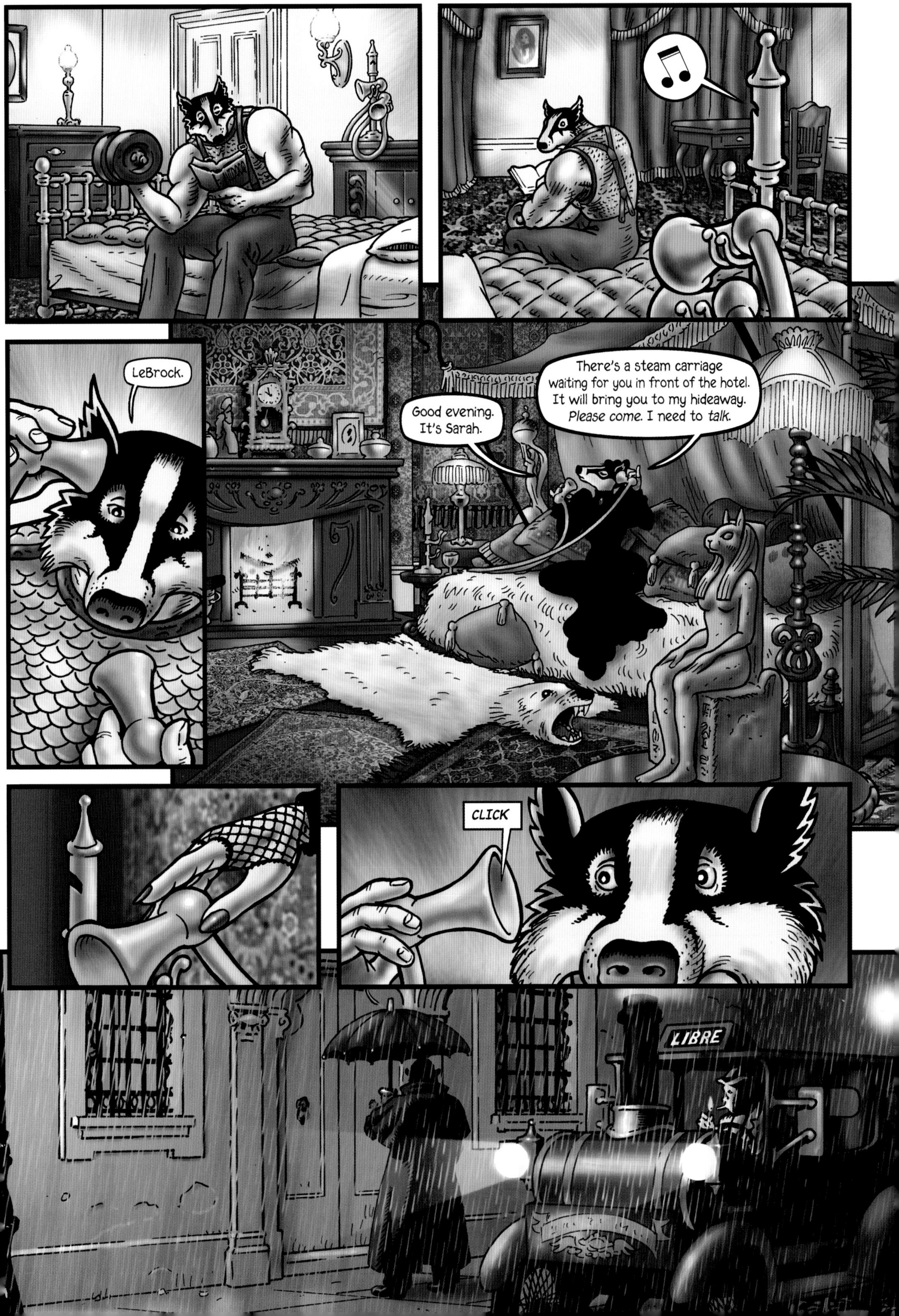
♫
LeBrock.
Good evening. It's Sarah.
There's a steam carriage waiting for you in front of the hotel. It will bring you to my hideaway. *Please come.* I need to *talk.*
CLICK
LIBRE

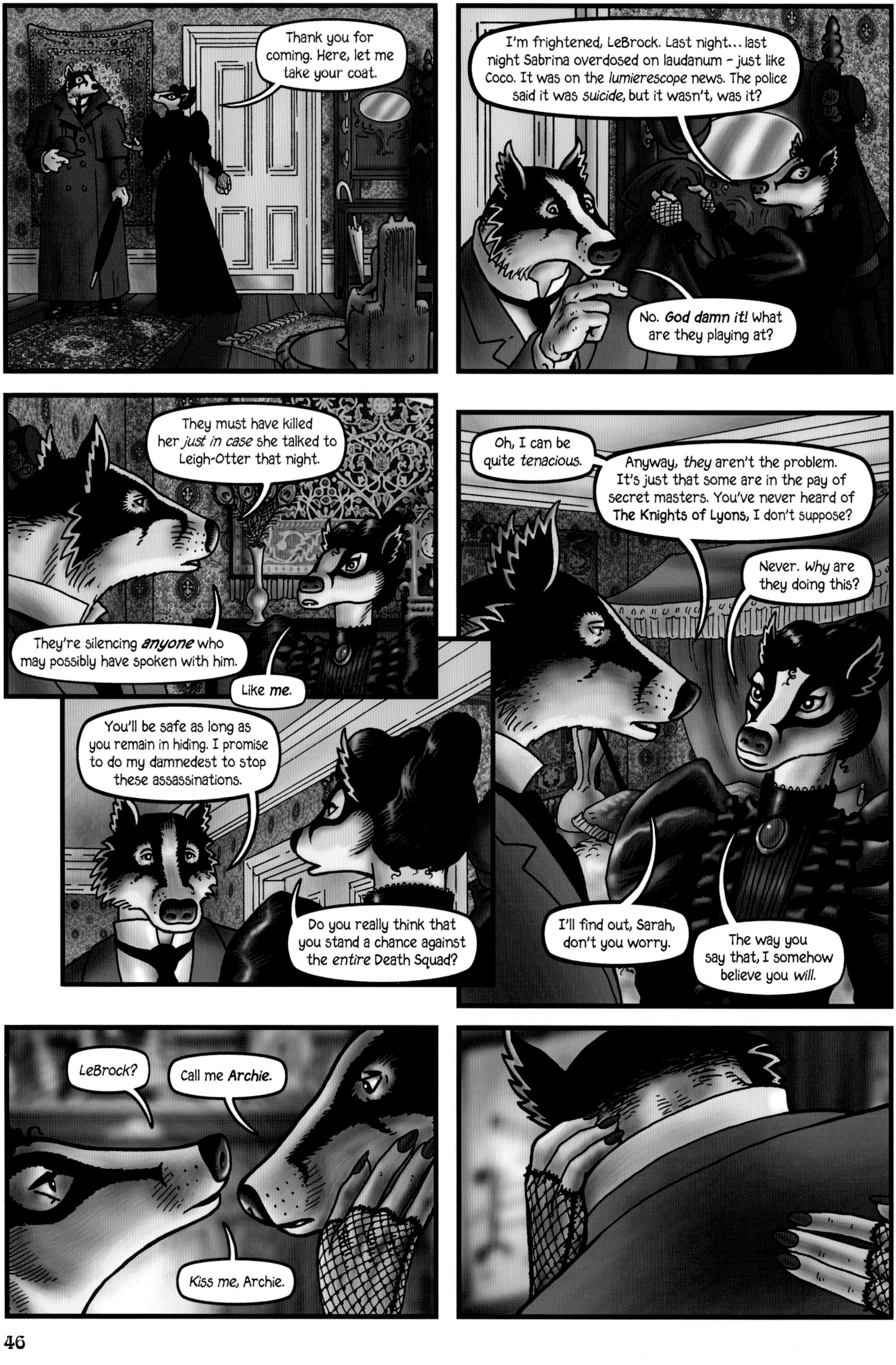

Thank you for coming. Here, let me take your coat.
I'm frightened, LeBrock. Last night... last night Sabrina overdosed on laudanum - just like Coco. It was on the *lumierescope* news. The police said it was *suicide*, but it wasn't, was it?
No. ***God damn it!*** What are they playing at?
They must have killed her *just in case* she talked to Leigh-Otter that night.
They're silencing ***anyone*** who may possibly have spoken with him.
Like ***me***.
You'll be safe as long as you remain in hiding. I promise to do my damnedest to stop these assassinations.
Do you really think that you stand a chance against the *entire* Death Squad?
Oh, I can be quite *tenacious*.
Anyway, *they* aren't the problem. It's just that some are in the pay of secret masters. You've never heard of **The Knights of Lyons**, I don't suppose?
Never. *Why* are they doing this?
I'll find out, Sarah, don't you worry.
The way you say that, I somehow believe you *will*.
LeBrock?
Call me **Archie**.
Kiss me, Archie.

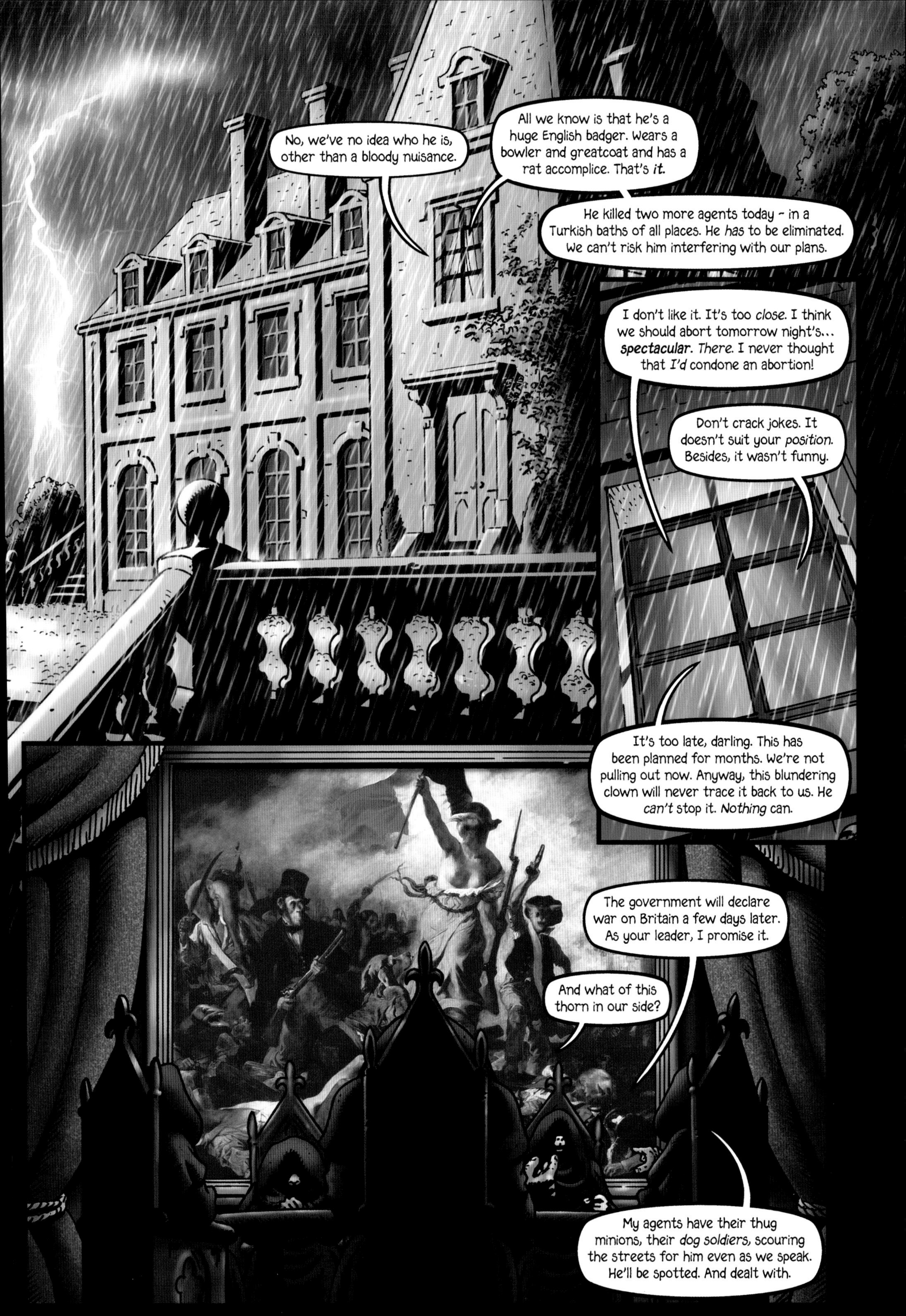

No, we've no idea who he is, other than a bloody nuisance.
All we know is that he's a huge English badger. Wears a bowler and greatcoat and has a rat accomplice. That's *it*.
He killed two more agents today - in a Turkish baths of all places. He *has* to be eliminated. We can't risk him interfering with our plans.
I don't like it. It's too *close*. I think we should abort tomorrow night's... **spectacular**. *There*. I never thought that *I'd* condone an abortion!
Don't crack jokes. It doesn't suit your *position*. Besides, it wasn't funny.
It's too late, darling. This has been planned for months. We're not pulling out now. Anyway, this blundering clown will never trace it back to us. He *can't* stop it. *Nothing* can.
The government will declare war on Britain a few days later. As your leader, I promise it.
And what of this thorn in our side?
My agents have their thug minions, their *dog soldiers*, scouring the streets for him even as we speak. He'll be spotted. And dealt with.

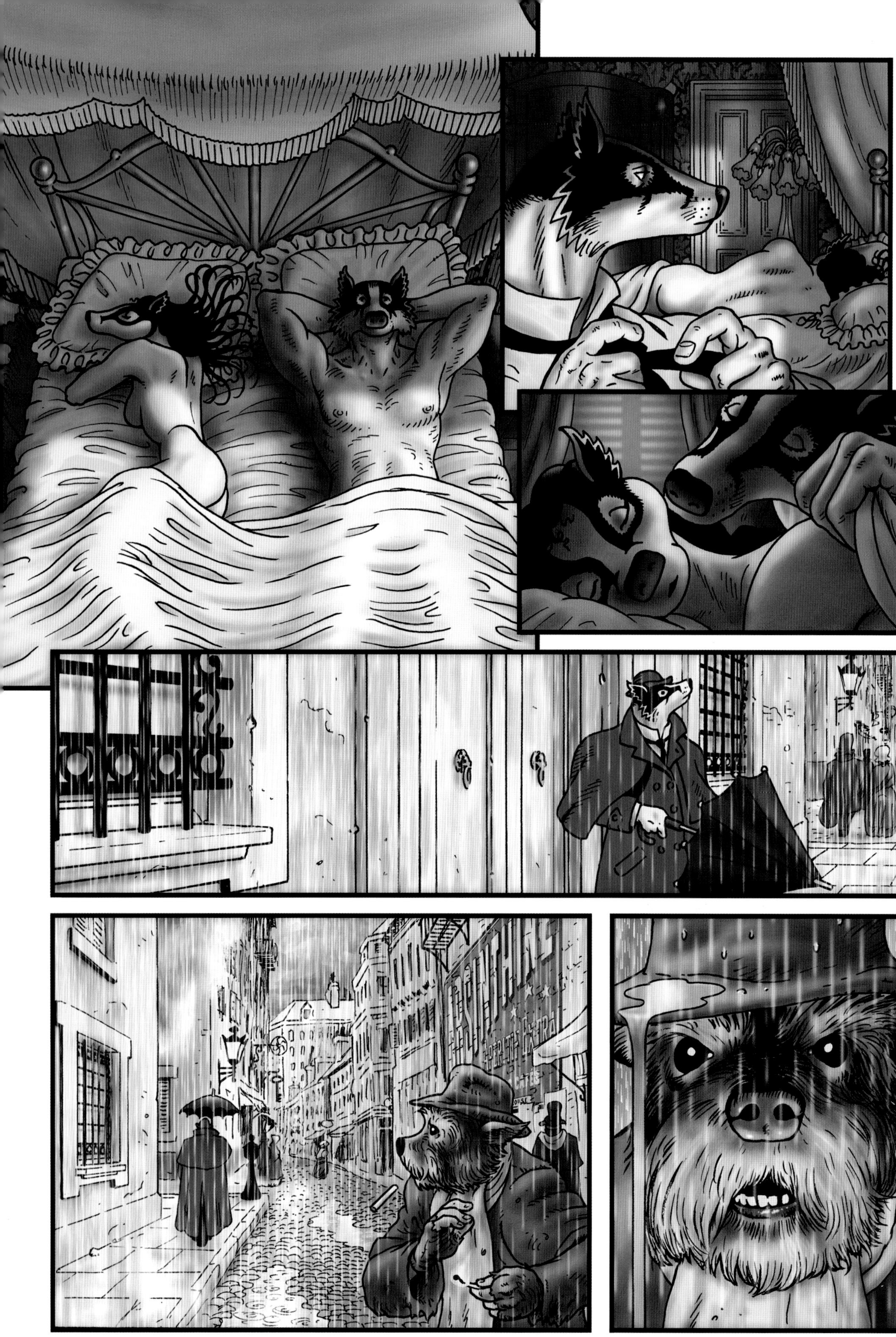
APÉRITIF EXTRA
CAFÉS

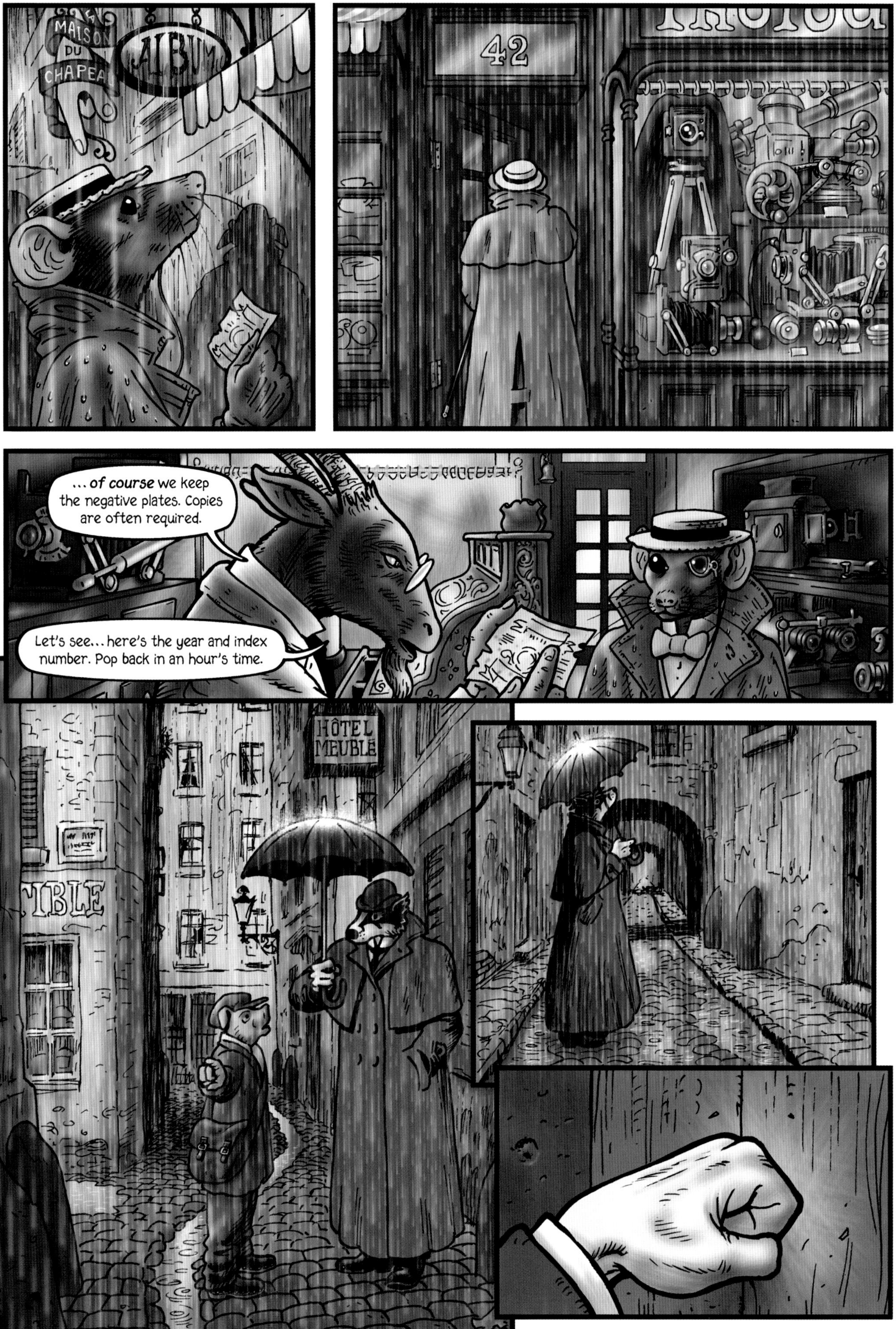
ALBUM
42
...*of course* we keep the negative plates. Copies are often required.
Let's see... here's the year and index number. Pop back in an hour's time.
HÔTEL MEUBLÉ

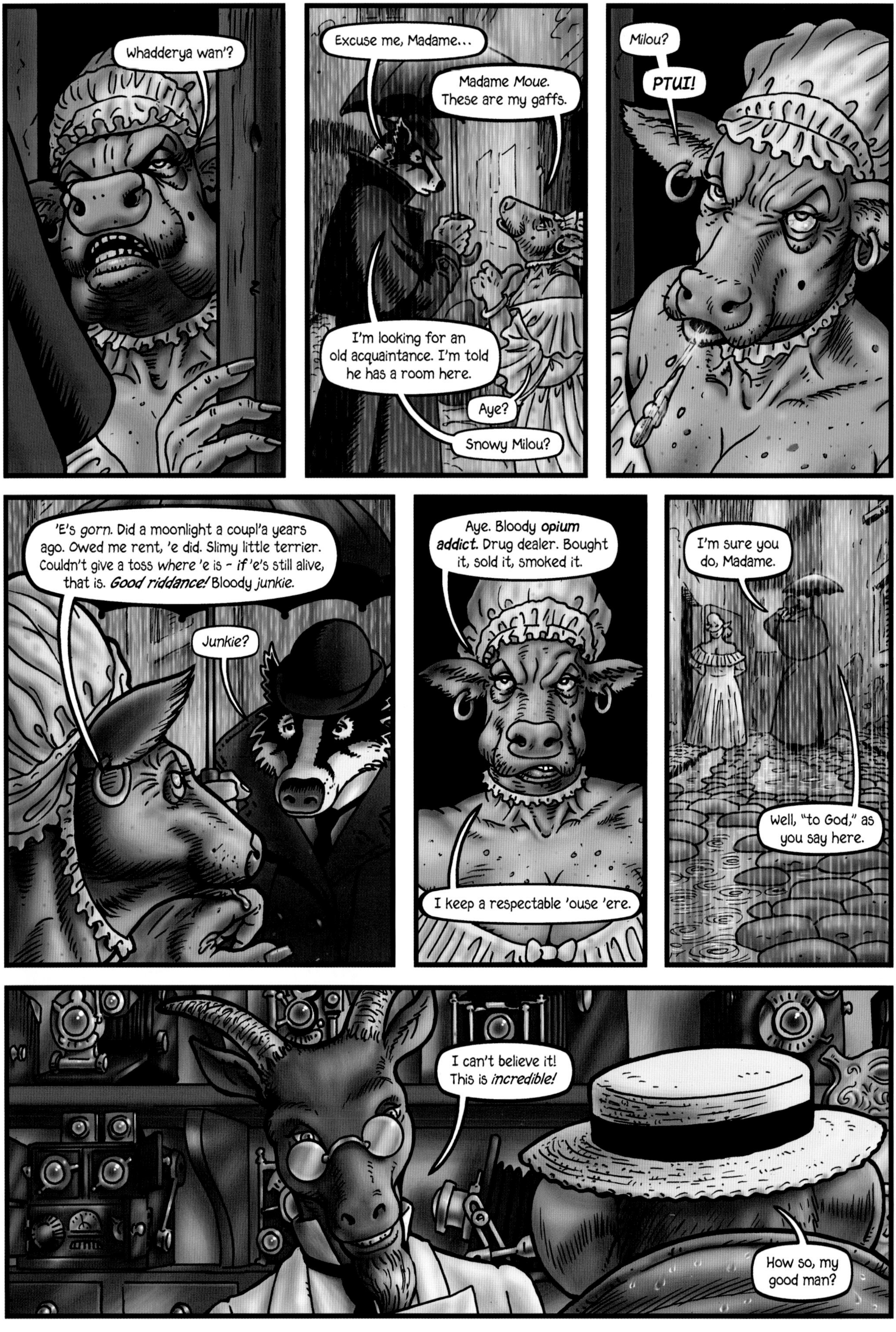
Whadderya wan'?
Excuse me, Madame...
Madame Moue. These are my gaffs.
I'm looking for an old acquaintance. I'm told he has a room here.
Aye?
Snowy Milou?
Milou?
PTUI!
'E's *gorn*. Did a moonlight a coupl'a years ago. Owed me rent, 'e did. Slimy little terrier. Couldn't give a toss *where* 'e is – *if* 'e's still alive, that is. *Good riddance!* Bloody *junkie*.
Junkie?
Aye. Bloody **opium addict**. Drug dealer. Bought it, sold it, smoked it.
I keep a respectable 'ouse 'ere.
I'm sure you do, Madame.
Well, "to God," as you say here.
I can't believe it! This is *incredible!*
How so, my good man?

Why, all of these people are *famous!*

Look, here's Professor Tope! And the Prime Minister! The War Minister! The Archbishop of Paris! The Chief of Police! And Madame Krupp herself!

What an *illustrious* hunting party!

If you say so, old bean. How much do I owe you?

This is very interesting.

I take it you noticed the year on the label from the picture frame?

Absolutely, DI. Two years ago.

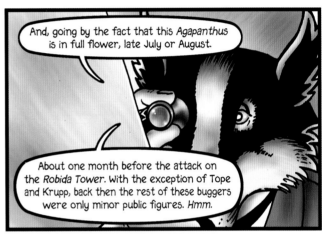

And, going by the fact that this *Agapanthus* is in full flower, late July or August.

About one month before the attack on the *Robida Tower.* With the exception of Tope and Krupp, back then the rest of these buggers were only minor public figures. *Hmm.*

Jean-Marie Lapin, now the Prime Minister, was simply the leader of a marginal far-right nationalist party. He shot to power in the elections following the Robida outrage – a landslide victory. What he promised was a "War on Terror" and a hard line against "British Anarchy."

His first act as PM was to appoint these three to key posts and pass several acts drastically curtailing civil liberties. Last year, he declared war on the *Communards* in French Indo-China.

But what does *this* have to do with Leigh-Otter, DI?

As a diplomat, he would have probably met one or more of them.

The Death Squad is a branch of the Secret Police. The Hyena there is their boss. I'll lay odds here are our *Knights of Lyons.*

Which do you think is the weakest link?

Let's start with the primate...

...after I've had a little talk with André Pegasus – *The Drug Baron of Paris.*

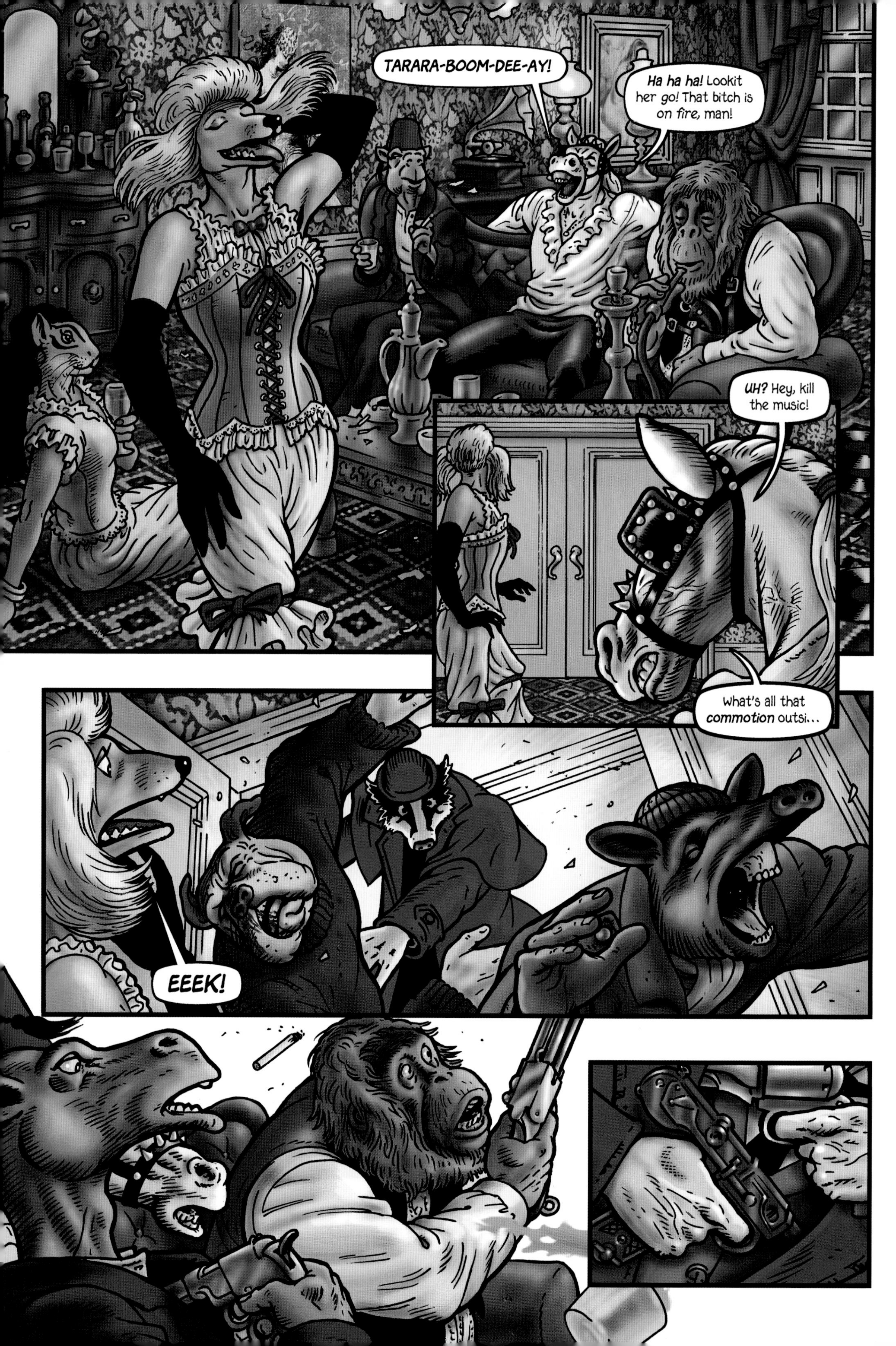
TARARA-BOOM-DEE-AY!
Ha ha ha! Lookit her go! That bitch is on fire, man!
UH? Hey, kill the music!
What's all that commotion outsi…
EEEK!

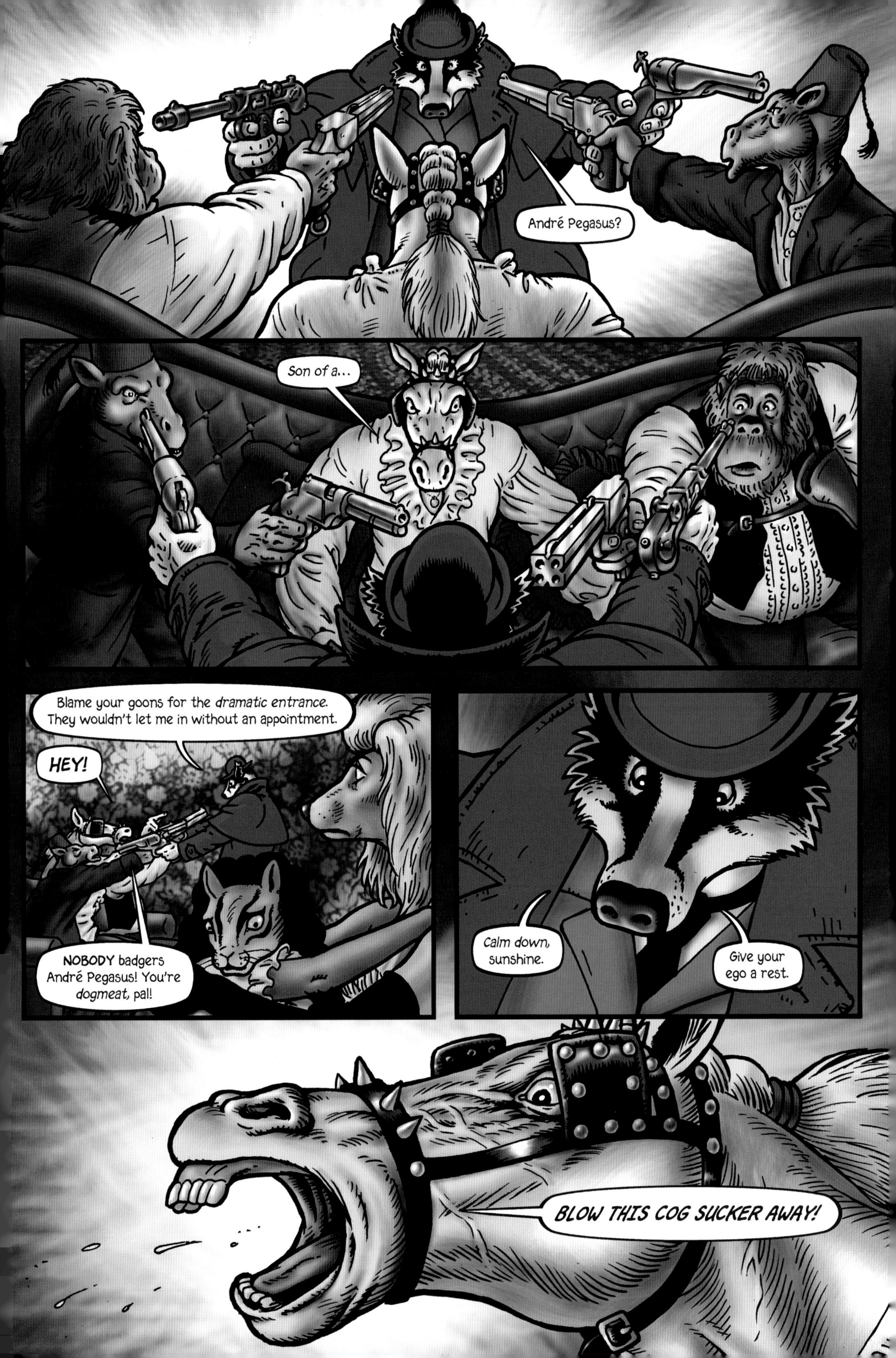
André Pegasus?
Son of a...
Blame your goons for the *dramatic entrance.* They wouldn't let me in without an appointment.
HEY!
NOBODY badgers André Pegasus! You're *dogmeat,* pal!
Calm down, sunshine.
Give your ego a rest.
BLOW THIS COG SUCKER AWAY!

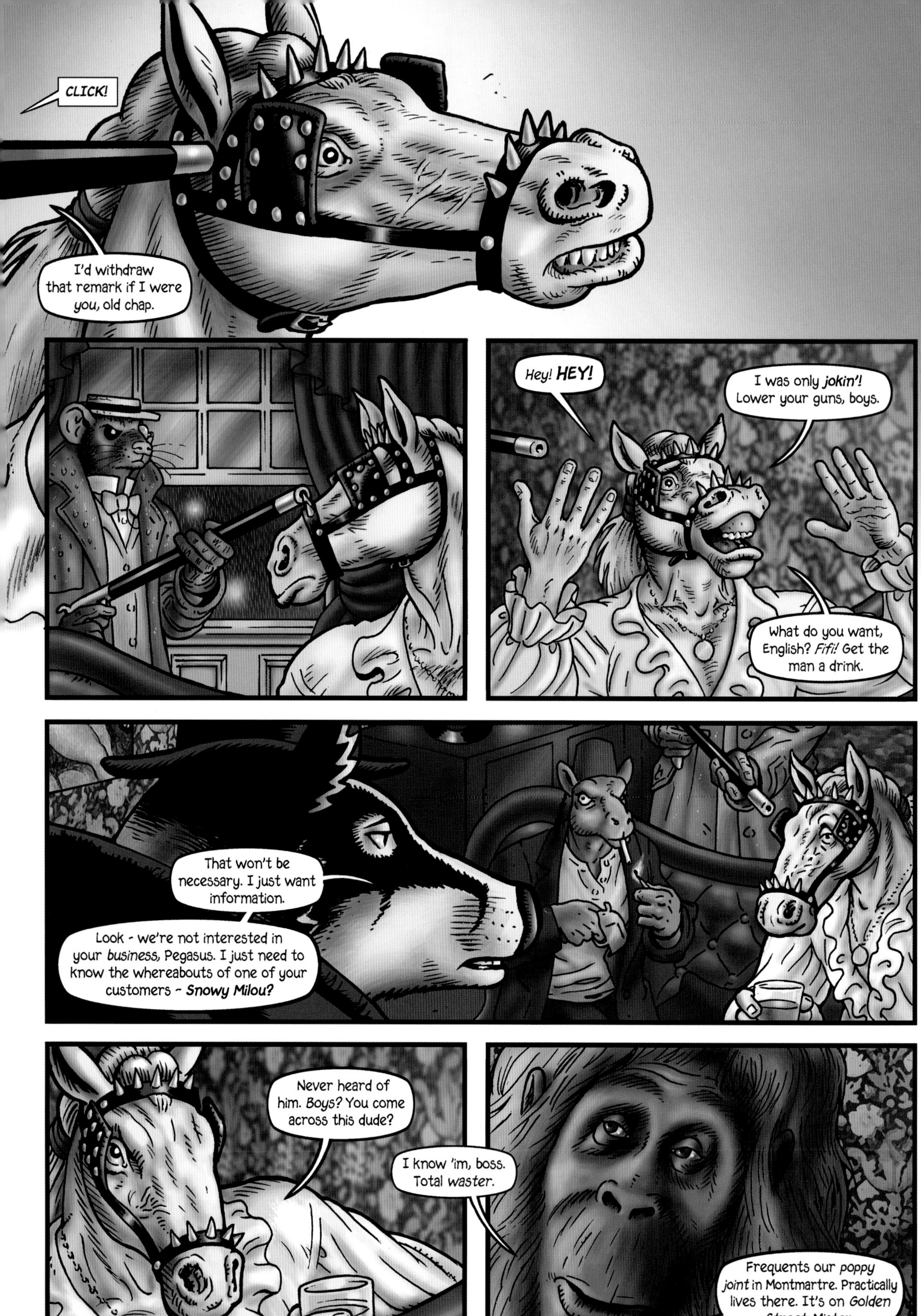
CLICK!
I'd withdraw that remark if I were *you*, old chap.
Hey! **HEY!**
I was only *jokin'!* Lower your guns, boys.
What do you want, English? *Fifi!* Get the man a drink.
That won't be necessary. I just want information.
Look - we're not interested in your *business*, Pegasus. I just need to know the whereabouts of one of your customers - **Snowy Milou?**
Never heard of him. *Boys?* You come across this dude?
I know 'im, boss. Total *waster*.
Frequents our *poppy joint* in Montmartre. Practically lives there. It's on *Golden Street*, Mister.

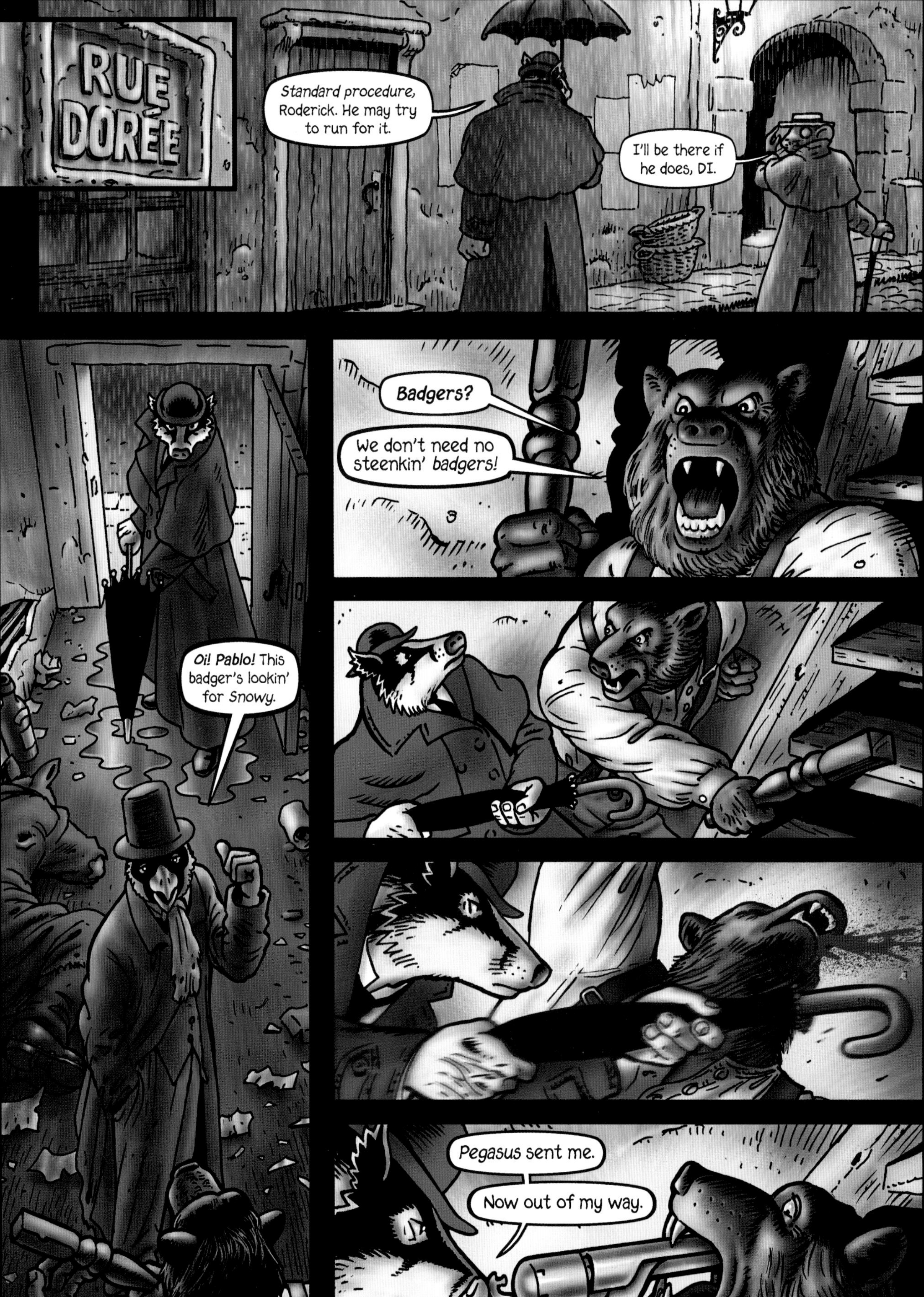
RUE DORÉE
Standard procedure, Roderick. He may try to run for it.
I'll be there if he does, DI.
Oi! Pablo! This badger's lookin' for *Snowy*.
Badgers?
We don't need no steenkin' *badgers!*
Pegasus sent me.
Now out of my way.

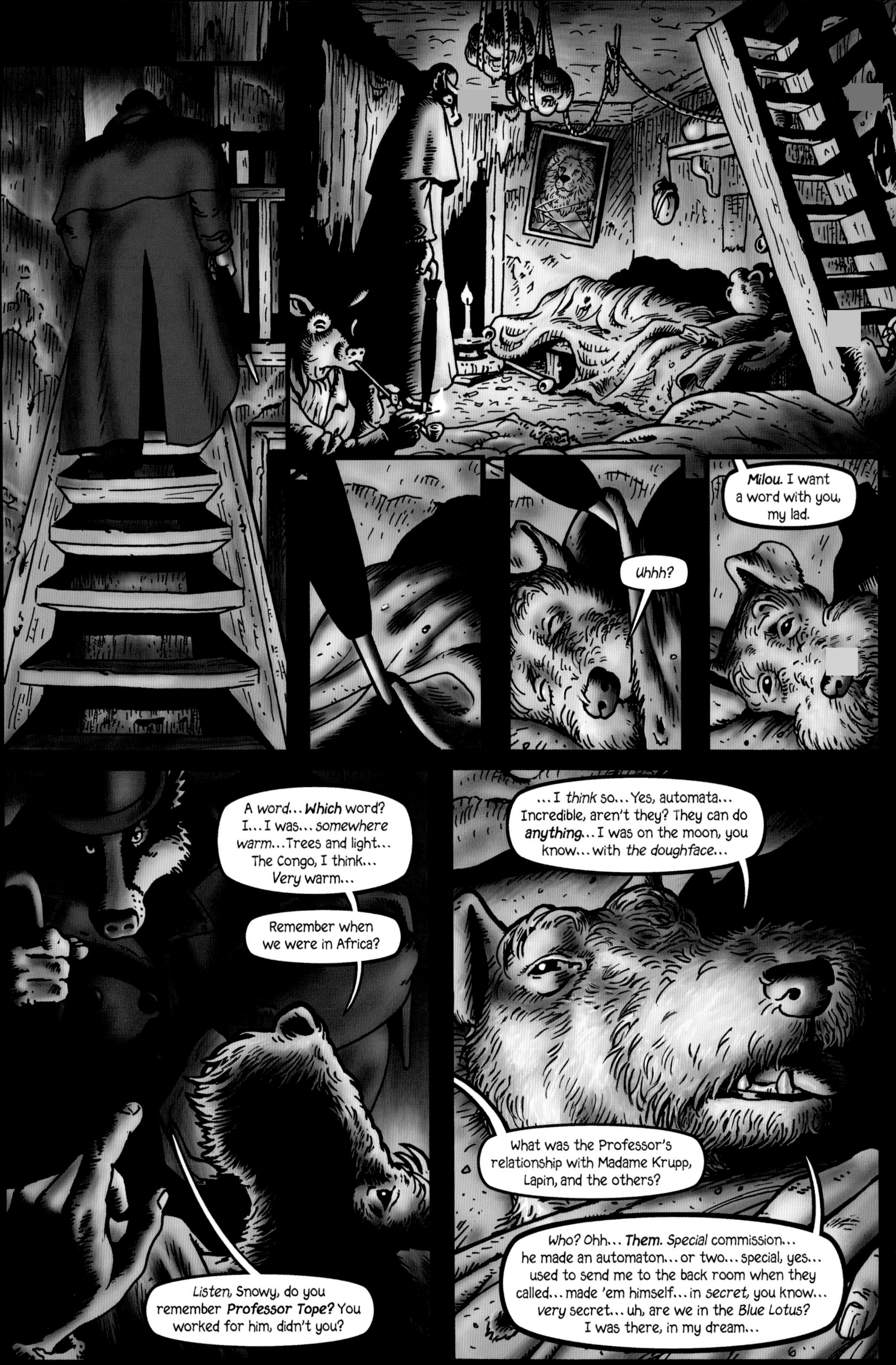
Milou. I want a word with you, my lad.
Uhhh?
A word... Which word? I... I was... somewhere warm... Trees and light... The Congo, I think... Very warm...
Remember when we were in Africa?
Listen, Snowy, do you remember Professor Tope? You worked for him, didn't you?
...I think so... Yes, automata... Incredible, aren't they? They can do anything... I was on the moon, you know... with the doughface...
What was the Professor's relationship with Madame Krupp, Lapin, and the others?
Who? Ohh... Them. Special commission... he made an automaton... or two... special, yes... used to send me to the back room when they called... made 'em himself... in secret, you know... very secret... uh, are we in the Blue Lotus? I was there, in my dream...

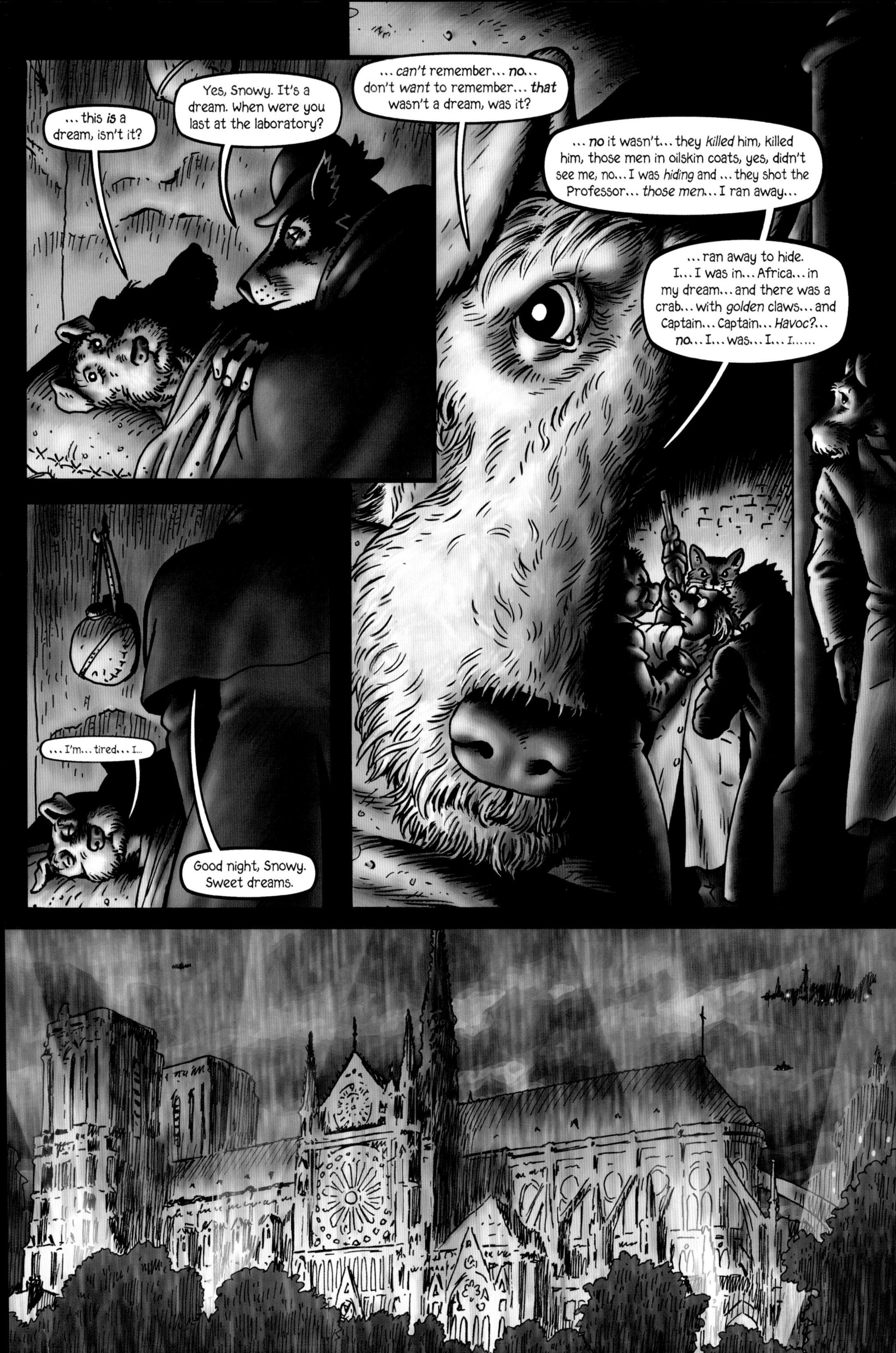
...this *is* a dream, isn't it?
Yes, Snowy. It's a dream. When were you last at the laboratory?
...*can't* remember... *no*... don't *want* to remember... *that* wasn't a dream, was it?
...*no* it wasn't... they *killed* him, killed him, those men in oilskin coats, yes, didn't see me, no... I was *hiding* and ... they shot the Professor... *those men*... I ran away...
...ran away to hide. I... I was in... Africa... in my dream... and there was a crab... with *golden* claws... and Captain... Captain... *Havoc?*... *no*... I... was... I... I......
...I'm... tired... I...
Good night, Snowy. Sweet dreams.

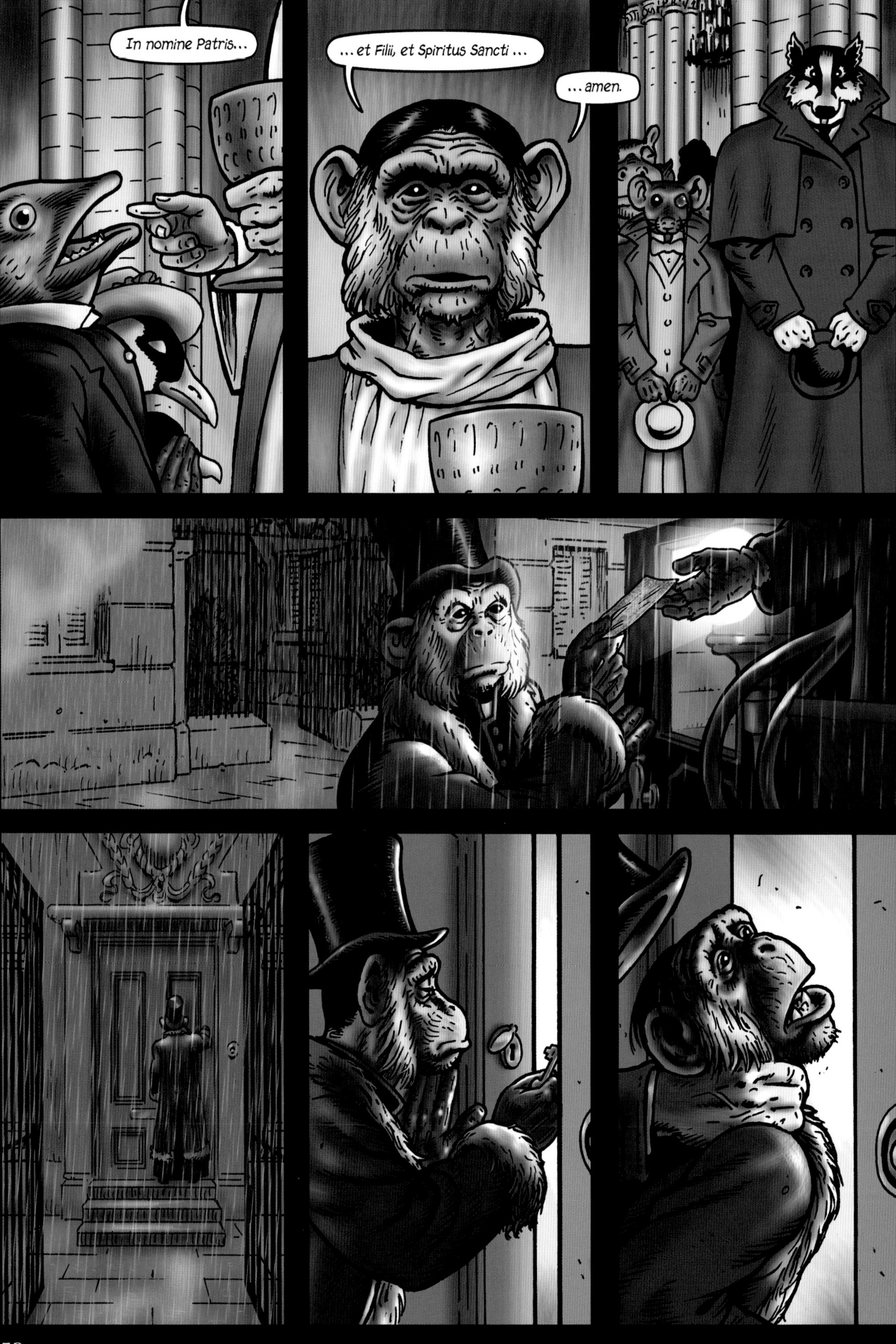
In nomine Patris...
...et Filii, et Spiritus Sancti ...
...amen.

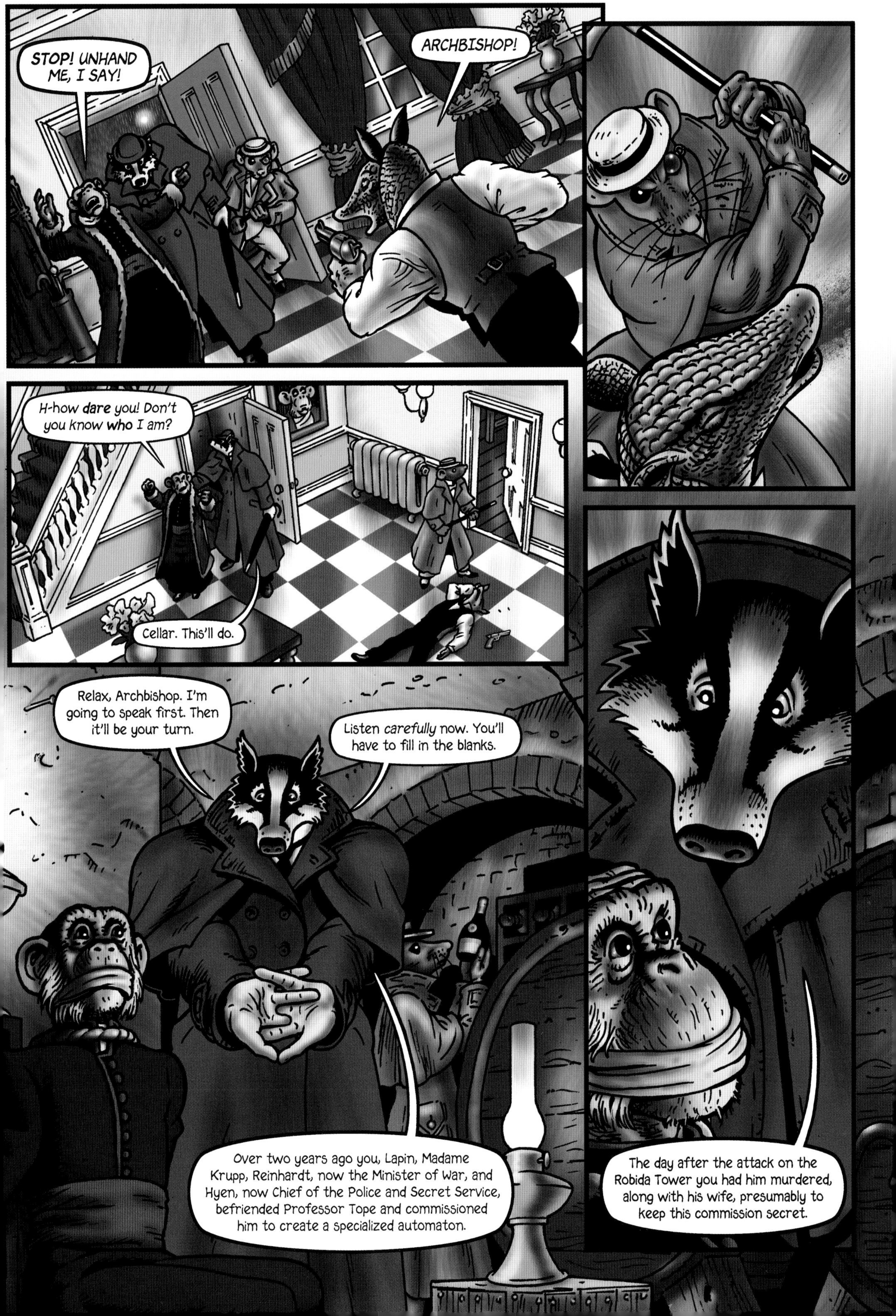
STOP! UNHAND ME, I SAY!
ARCHBISHOP!
H-how **dare** you! Don't you know **who** I am?
Cellar. This'll do.
Relax, Archbishop. I'm going to speak first. Then it'll be your turn.
Listen *carefully* now. You'll have to fill in the blanks.
Over two years ago you, Lapin, Madame Krupp, Reinhardt, now the Minister of War, and Hyen, now Chief of the Police and Secret Service, befriended Professor Tope and commissioned him to create a specialized automaton.
The day after the attack on the Robida Tower you had him murdered, along with his wife, presumably to keep this commission secret.

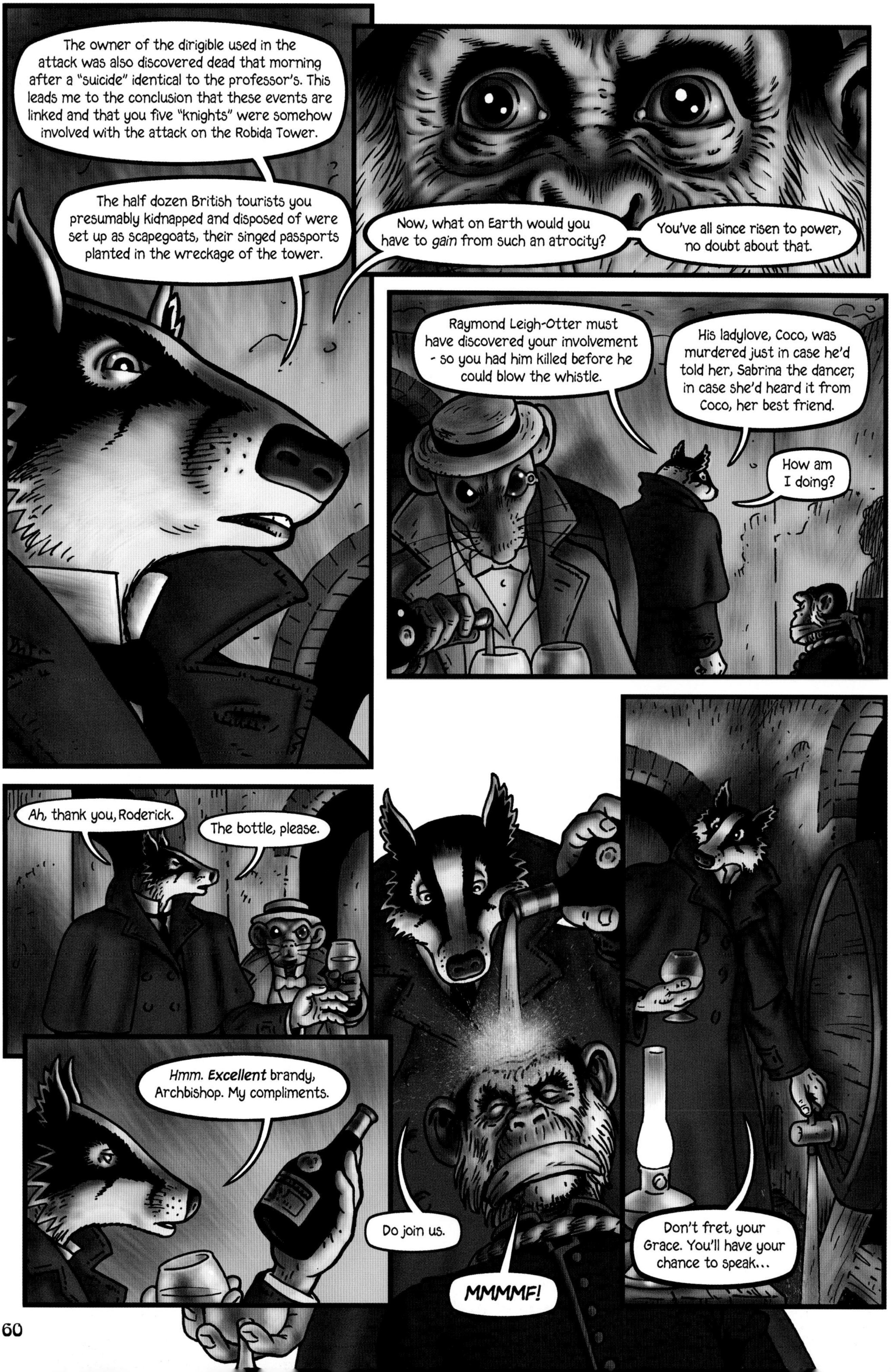

The owner of the dirigible used in the attack was also discovered dead that morning after a "suicide" identical to the professor's. This leads me to the conclusion that these events are linked and that you five "knights" were somehow involved with the attack on the Robida Tower.
The half dozen British tourists you presumably kidnapped and disposed of were set up as scapegoats, their singed passports planted in the wreckage of the tower.
Now, what on Earth would you have to *gain* from such an atrocity?
You've all since risen to power, no doubt about that.
Raymond Leigh-Otter must have discovered your involvement - so you had him killed before he could blow the whistle.
His ladylove, Coco, was murdered just in case he'd told her, Sabrina the dancer, in case she'd heard it from Coco, her best friend.
How am I doing?
Ah, thank you, Roderick.
The bottle, please.
Hmm. ***Excellent*** brandy, Archbishop. My compliments.
Do join us.
MMMMF!
Don't fret, your Grace. You'll have your chance to speak...

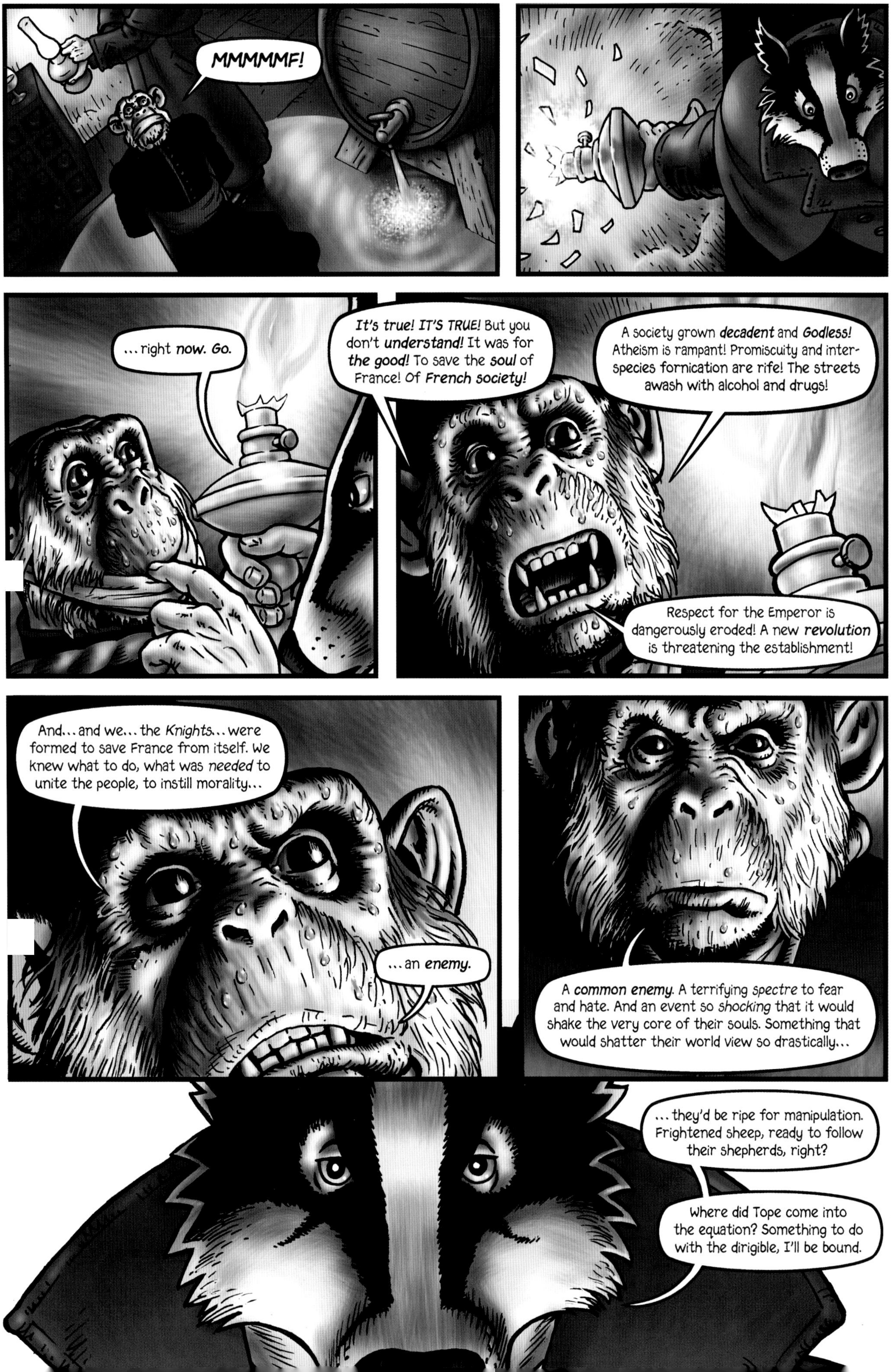
MMMMMF!
...right now. Go.
It's true! IT'S TRUE! But you don't understand! It was for the good! To save the soul of France! Of French society!
A society grown decadent and Godless! Atheism is rampant! Promiscuity and inter-species fornication are rife! The streets awash with alcohol and drugs!
Respect for the Emperor is dangerously eroded! A new revolution is threatening the establishment!
And...and we...the Knights...were formed to save France from itself. We knew what to do, what was needed to unite the people, to instill morality...
...an enemy.
A common enemy. A terrifying spectre to fear and hate. And an event so shocking that it would shake the very core of their souls. Something that would shatter their world view so drastically...
...they'd be ripe for manipulation. Frightened sheep, ready to follow their shepherds, right?
Where did Tope come into the equation? Something to do with the dirigible, I'll be bound.

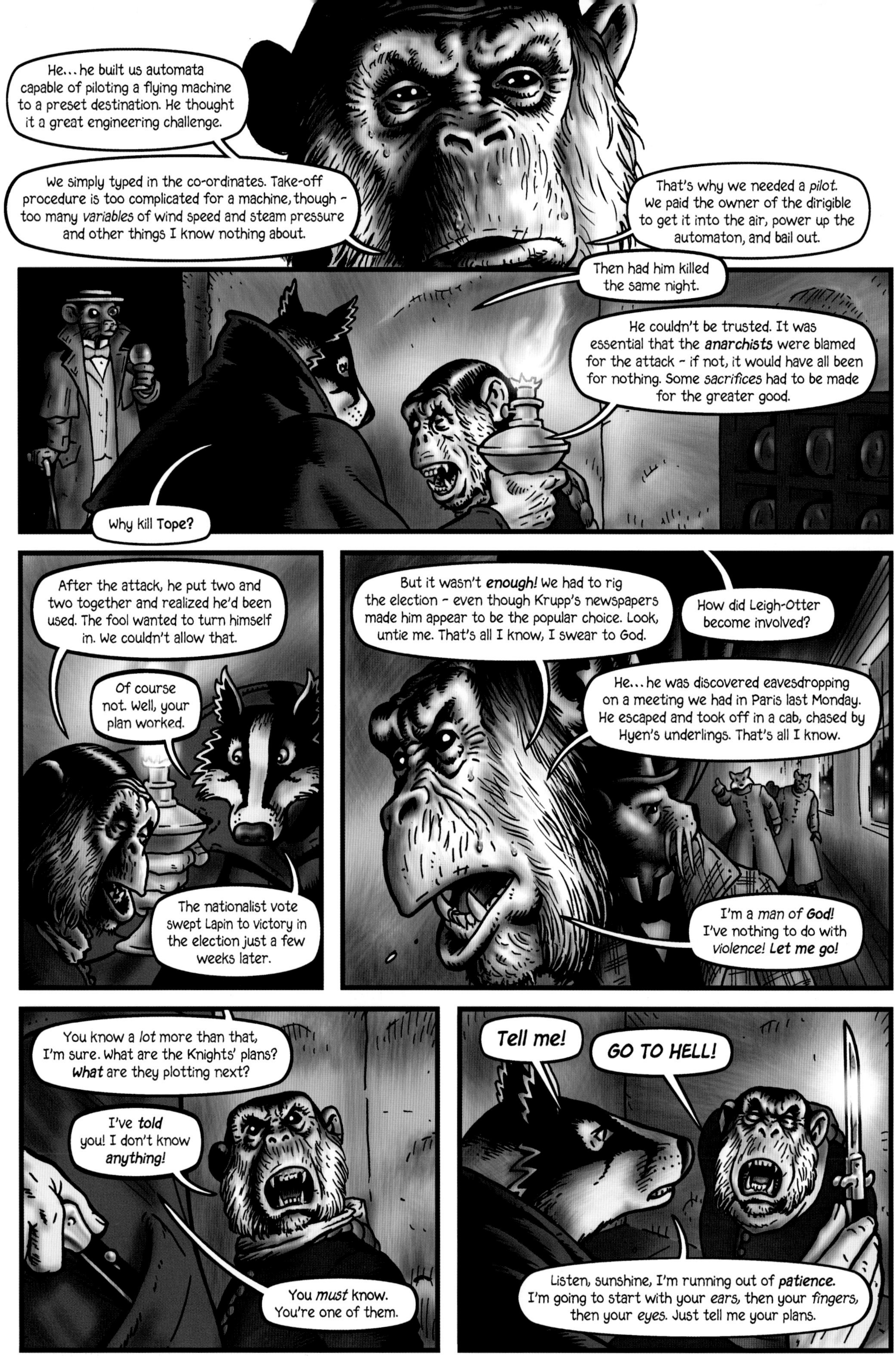
He... he built us automata capable of piloting a flying machine to a preset destination. He thought it a great engineering challenge.
We simply typed in the co-ordinates. Take-off procedure is too complicated for a machine, though - too many *variables* of wind speed and steam pressure and other things I know nothing about.
That's why we needed a *pilot*. We paid the owner of the dirigible to get it into the air, power up the automaton, and bail out.
Then had him killed the same night.
He couldn't be trusted. It was essential that the **anarchists** were blamed for the attack - if not, it would have all been for nothing. Some *sacrifices* had to be made for the greater good.
Why kill **Tope?**
After the attack, he put two and two together and realized he'd been used. The fool wanted to turn himself in. We couldn't allow that.
Of course not. Well, your plan worked.
The nationalist vote swept Lapin to victory in the election just a few weeks later.
But it wasn't ***enough!*** We had to rig the election - even though Krupp's newspapers made him appear to be the popular choice. Look, untie me. That's all I know, I swear to God.
How did Leigh-Otter become involved?
He... he was discovered eavesdropping on a meeting we had in Paris last Monday. He escaped and took off in a cab, chased by Hyen's underlings. That's all I know.
I'm a *man of **God!*** I've nothing to do with *violence!* ***Let me go!***
You know a *lot* more than that, I'm sure. What are the Knights' plans? ***What*** are they plotting next?
I've ***told*** you! I don't know ***anything!***
You *must* know. You're one of them.
Tell me!
GO TO HELL!
Listen, sunshine, I'm running out of ***patience.*** I'm going to start with your *ears*, then your *fingers*, then your *eyes*. Just tell me your plans.

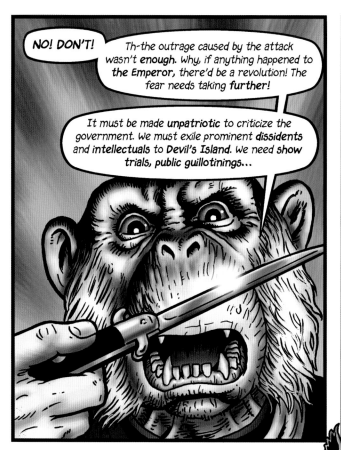

NO! DON'T!

Th-the outrage caused by the attack wasn't **enough**. Why, if anything happened to **the Emperor**, there'd be a revolution! The fear needs taking **further**!

It must be made **unpatriotic** to criticize the government. We must exile prominent **dissidents** and **intellectuals** to **Devil's Island**. We need show trials, public guillotinings...

PLANS! THE FACTS! NOW!

STOP!

Look - the war in **Indo-china** didn't unite the nation as we **hoped**. We need a more **immediate** threat. Just **one** more outrageous **act of terror** followed by the news that London is about to launch its **super-bomb** at Paris and we'll have **full public backing** for a war on Britain!

WHAT ACT OF TERROR? WHEN?

I DON'T KNOW!

AAAARGH!

T-TOMORROW NIGHT! THEY'RE LAUNCHING ANOTHER SKYSHIP FROM KRUPP'S ESTATE!

What's the target?

THE PARIS OPERA HOUSE! THE **TRANS-EMPIRE SONG CONTEST!** THERE'LL BE THOUSANDS THERE!

Thanks. C'mon, Roderick.

Y-YOU BASTARD! DON'T LEAVE ME LIKE **THIS!**

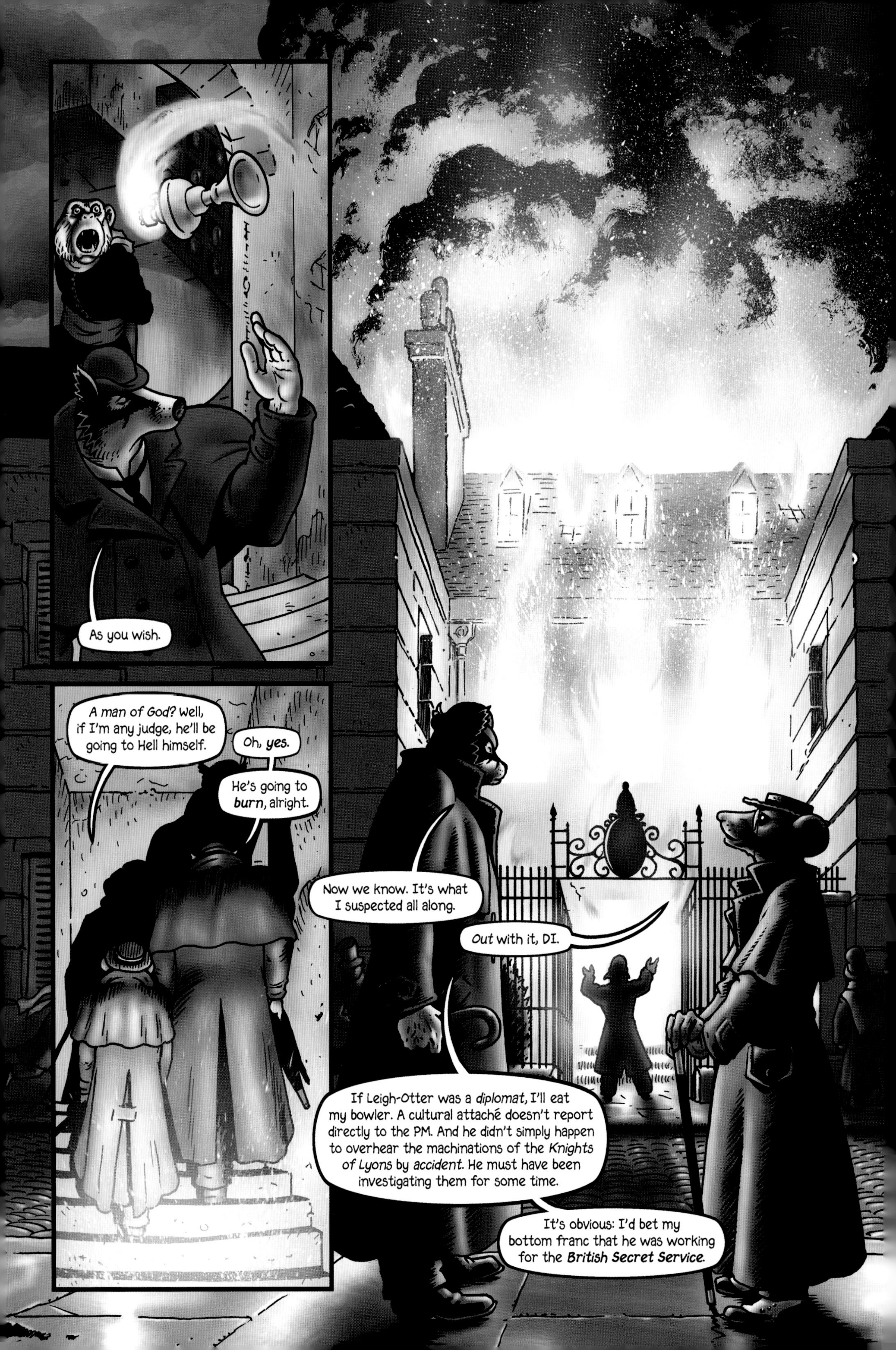
As you wish.
A man of God? Well, if I'm any judge, he'll be going to Hell himself.
Oh, yes.
He's going to burn, alright.
Now we know. It's what I suspected all along.
Out with it, DI.
If Leigh-Otter was a diplomat, I'll eat my bowler. A cultural attaché doesn't report directly to the PM. And he didn't simply happen to overhear the machinations of the Knights of Lyons by accident. He must have been investigating them for some time.
It's obvious: I'd bet my bottom franc that he was working for the British Secret Service.

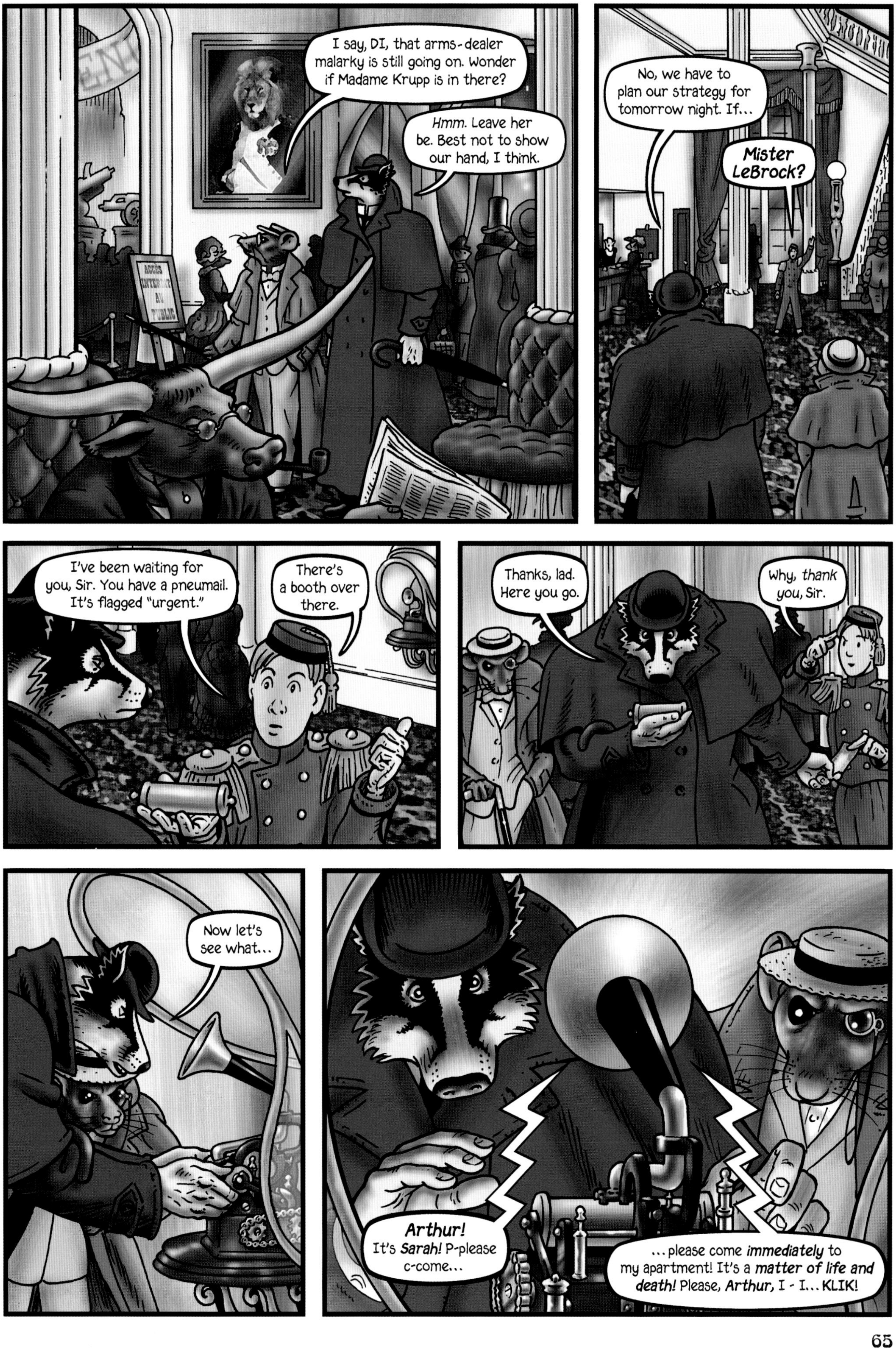
I say, DI, that arms-dealer malarky is still going on. Wonder if Madame Krupp is in there?
Hmm. Leave her be. Best not to show our hand, I think.
ACCÈS INTERDIT AU PUBLIC
No, we have to plan our strategy for tomorrow night. If...
Mister LeBrock?
I've been waiting for you, Sir. You have a pneumail. It's flagged "urgent."
There's a booth over there.
Thanks, lad. Here you go.
Why, thank you, Sir.
Now let's see what...
Arthur! It's Sarah! P-please c-come...
...please come immediately to my apartment! It's a matter of life and death! Please, Arthur, I - I... KLIK!

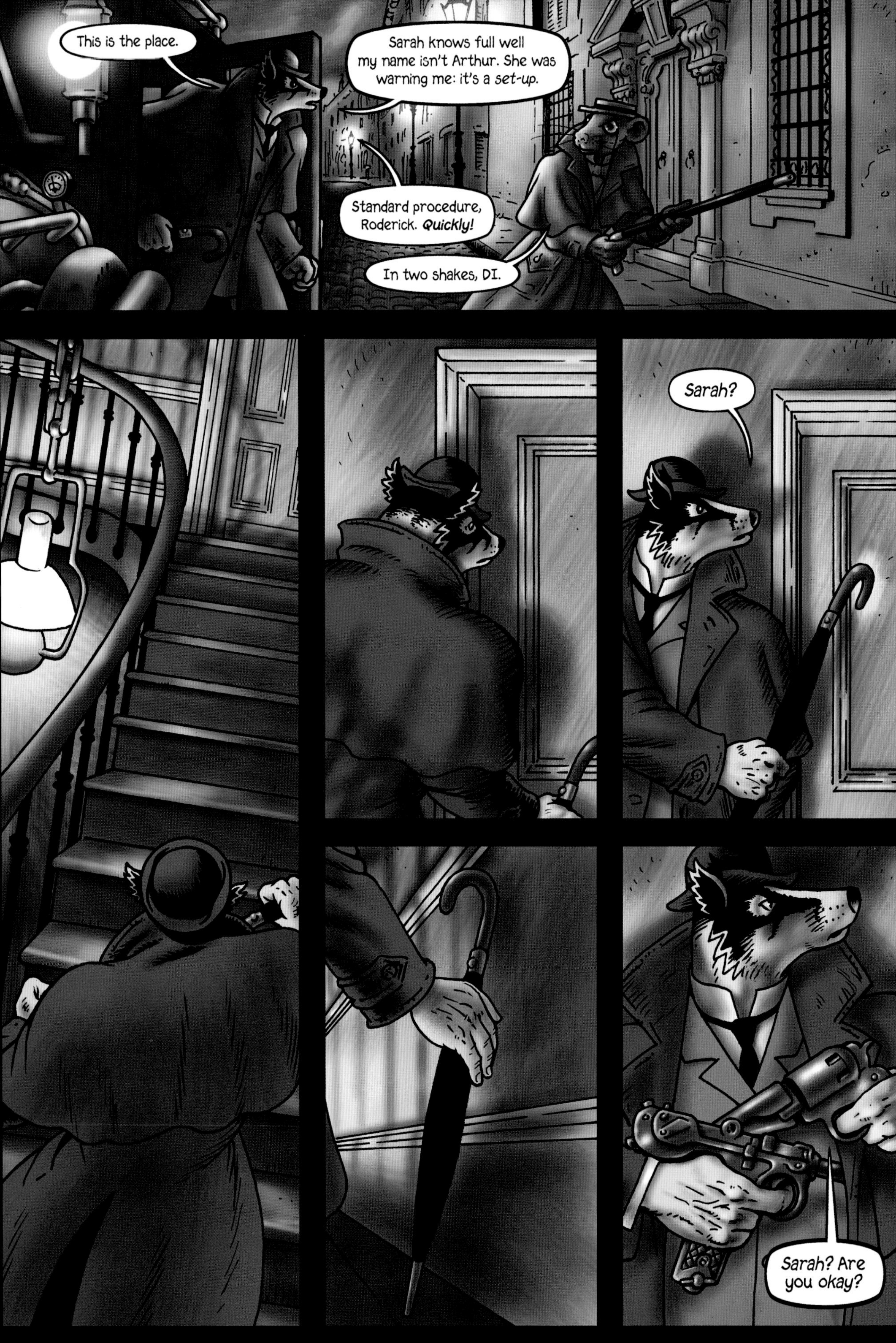
This is the place.
Sarah knows full well my name isn't Arthur. She was warning me: it's a *set-up*.
Standard procedure, Roderick. ***Quickly!***
In two shakes, DI.
Sarah?
Sarah? Are you okay?

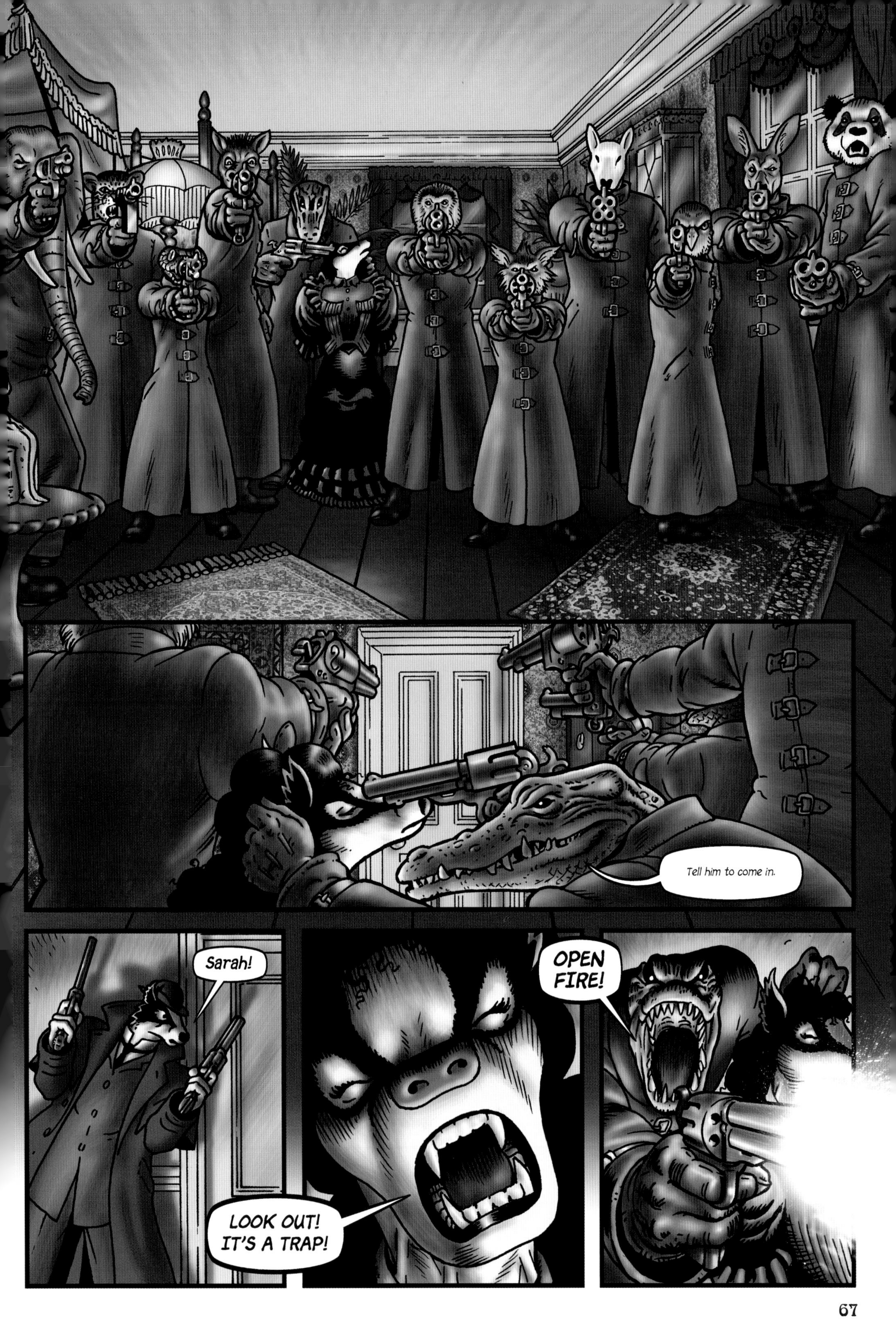
Tell him to come in.
Sarah!
LOOK OUT! IT'S A TRAP!
OPEN FIRE!

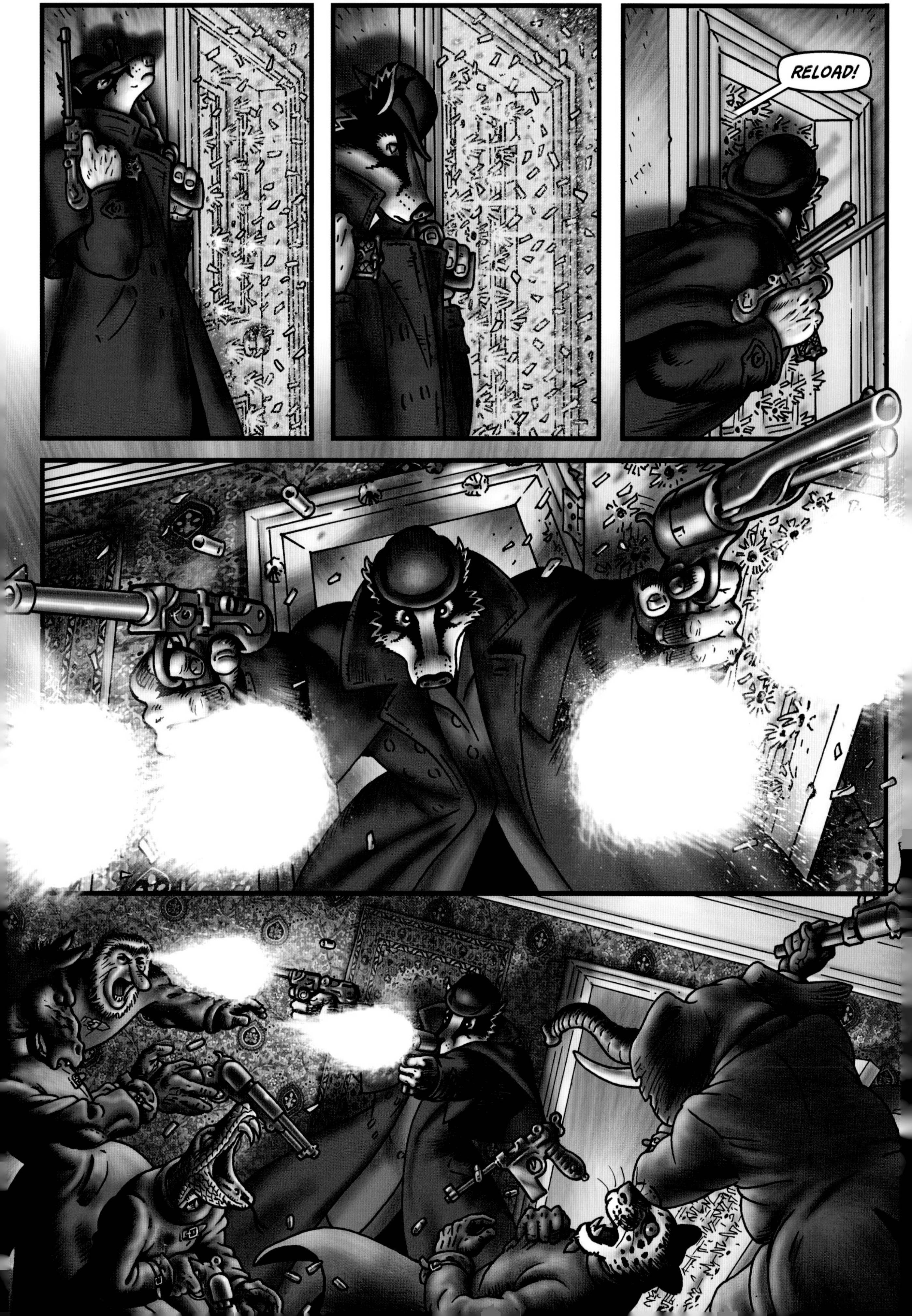
RELOAD!

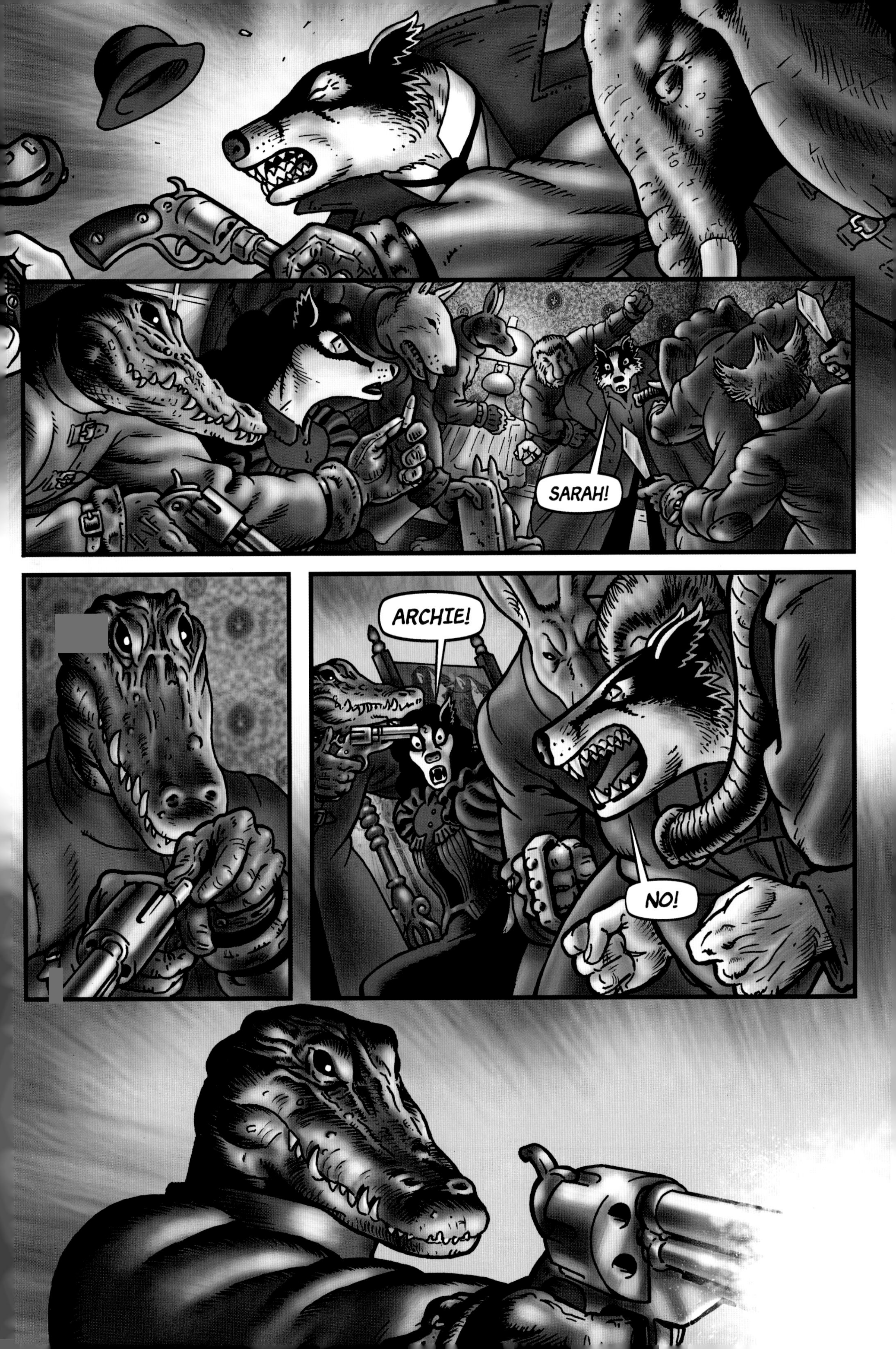
SARAH!
ARCHIE!
NO!

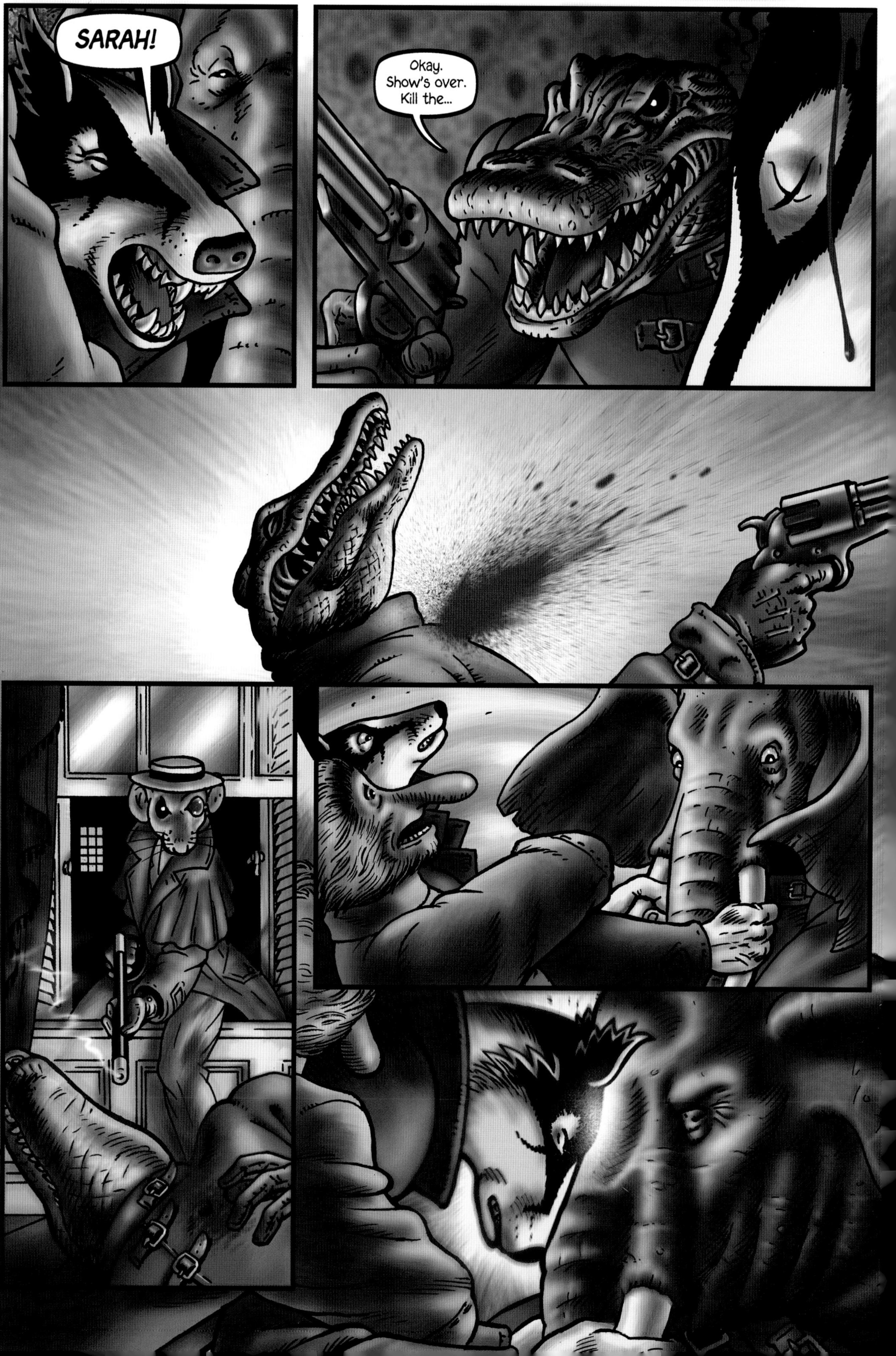
SARAH!
Okay. Show's over. Kill the...

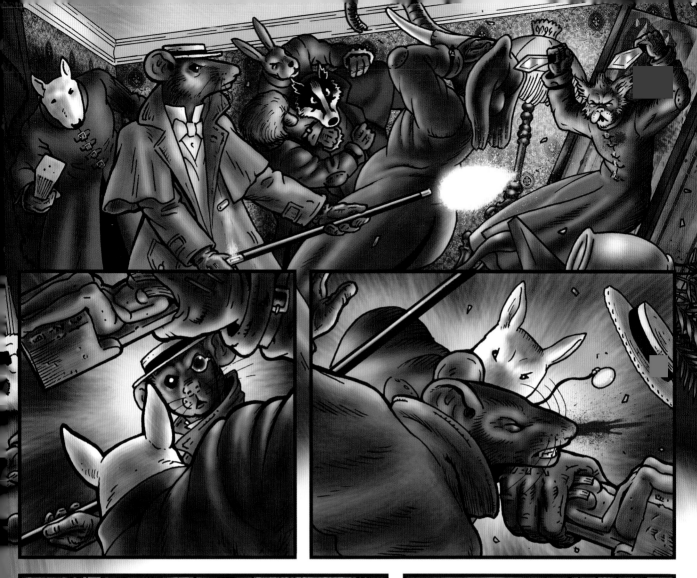

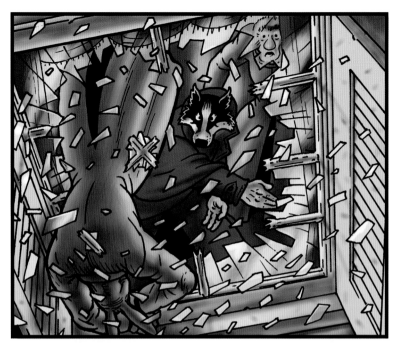

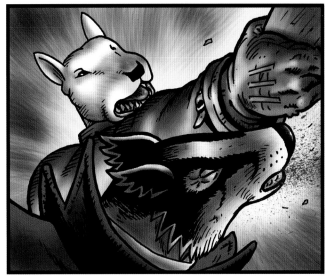

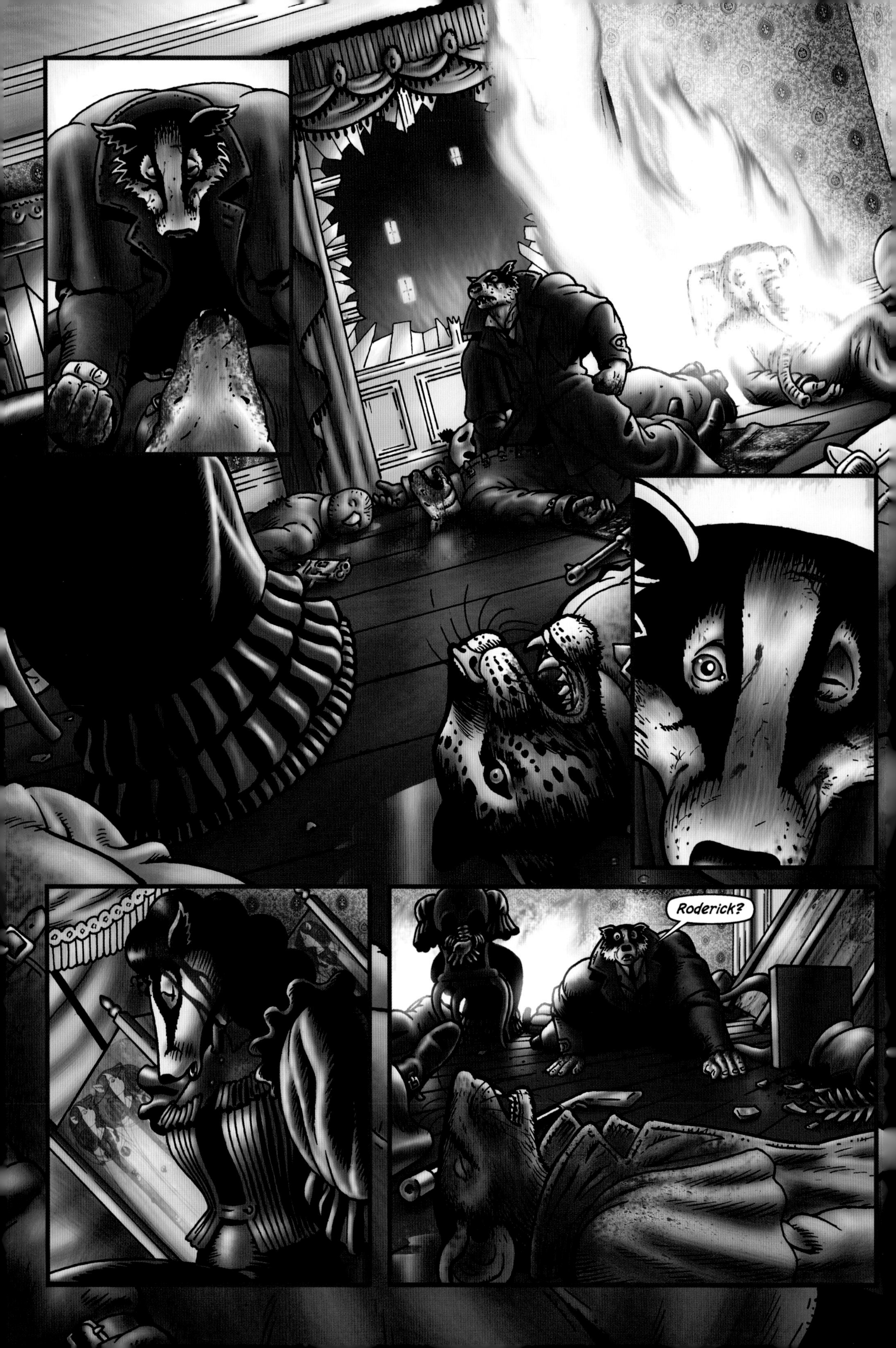
Roderick?

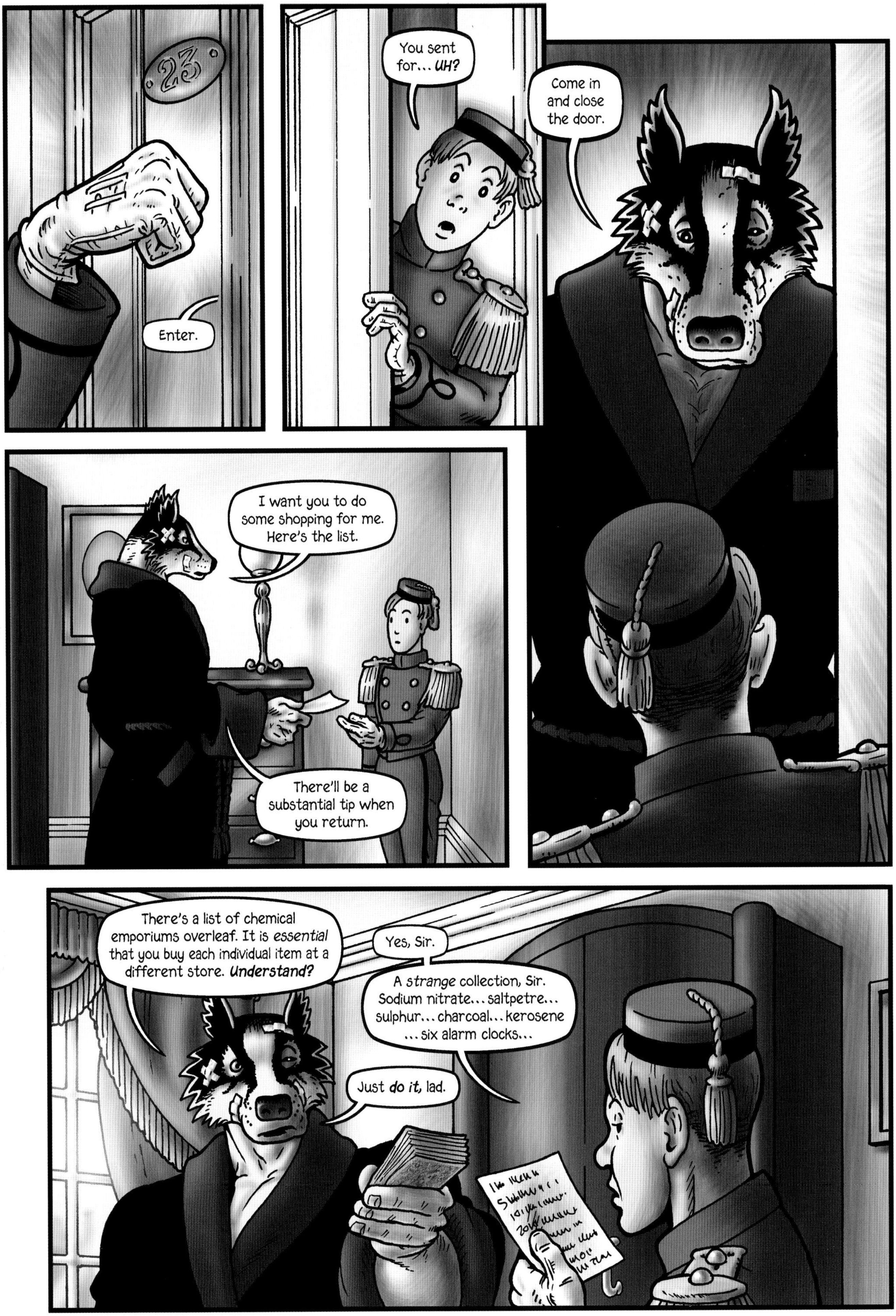

23
Enter.
You sent for... *UH?*
Come in and close the door.
I want you to do some shopping for me. Here's the list.
There'll be a substantial tip when you return.
There's a list of chemical emporiums overleaf. It is *essential* that you buy each individual item at a different store. ***Understand?***
Yes, Sir.
A *strange* collection, Sir. Sodium nitrate... saltpetre... sulphur... charcoal... kerosene ... six alarm clocks...
Just ***do it,*** lad.

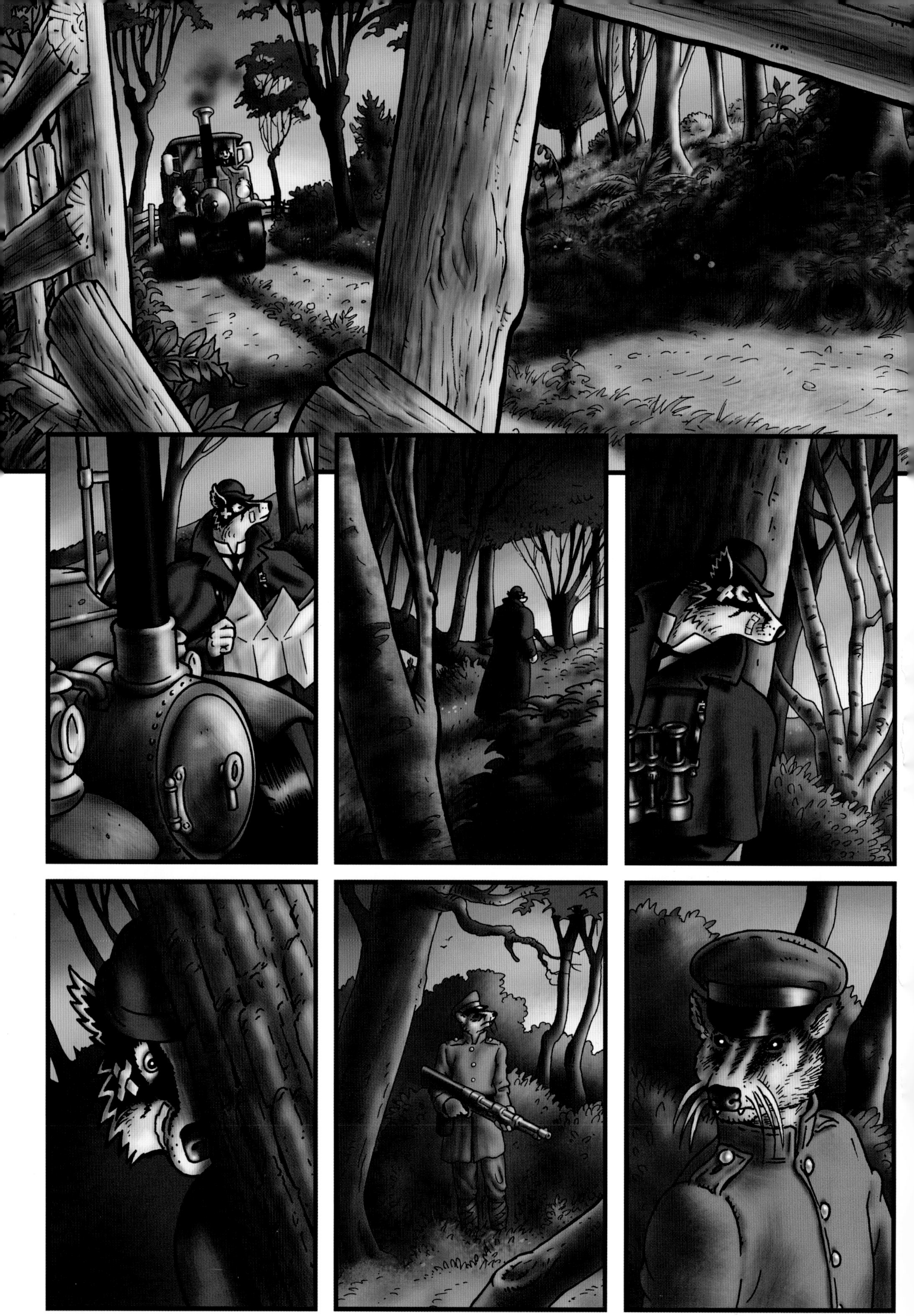

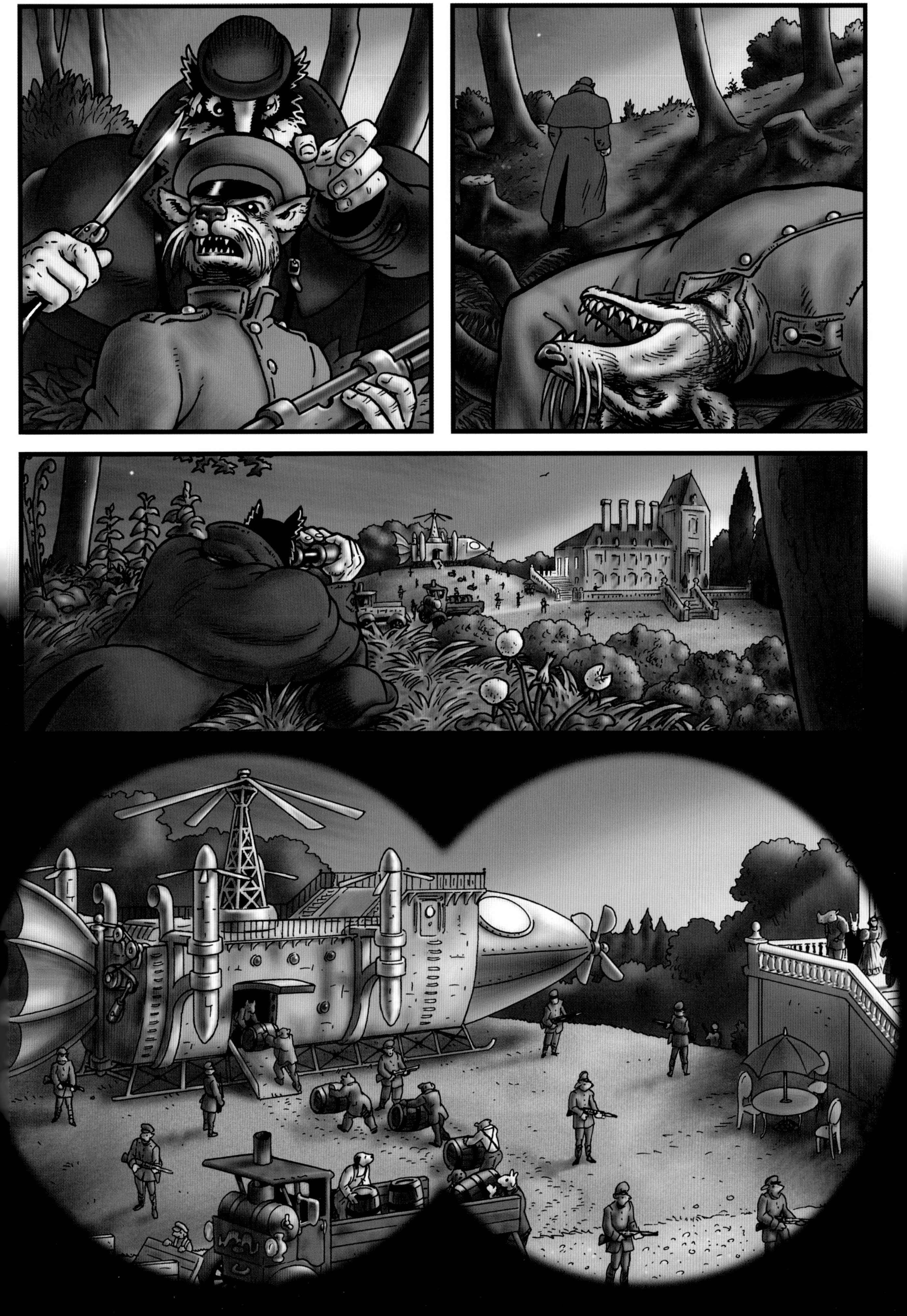

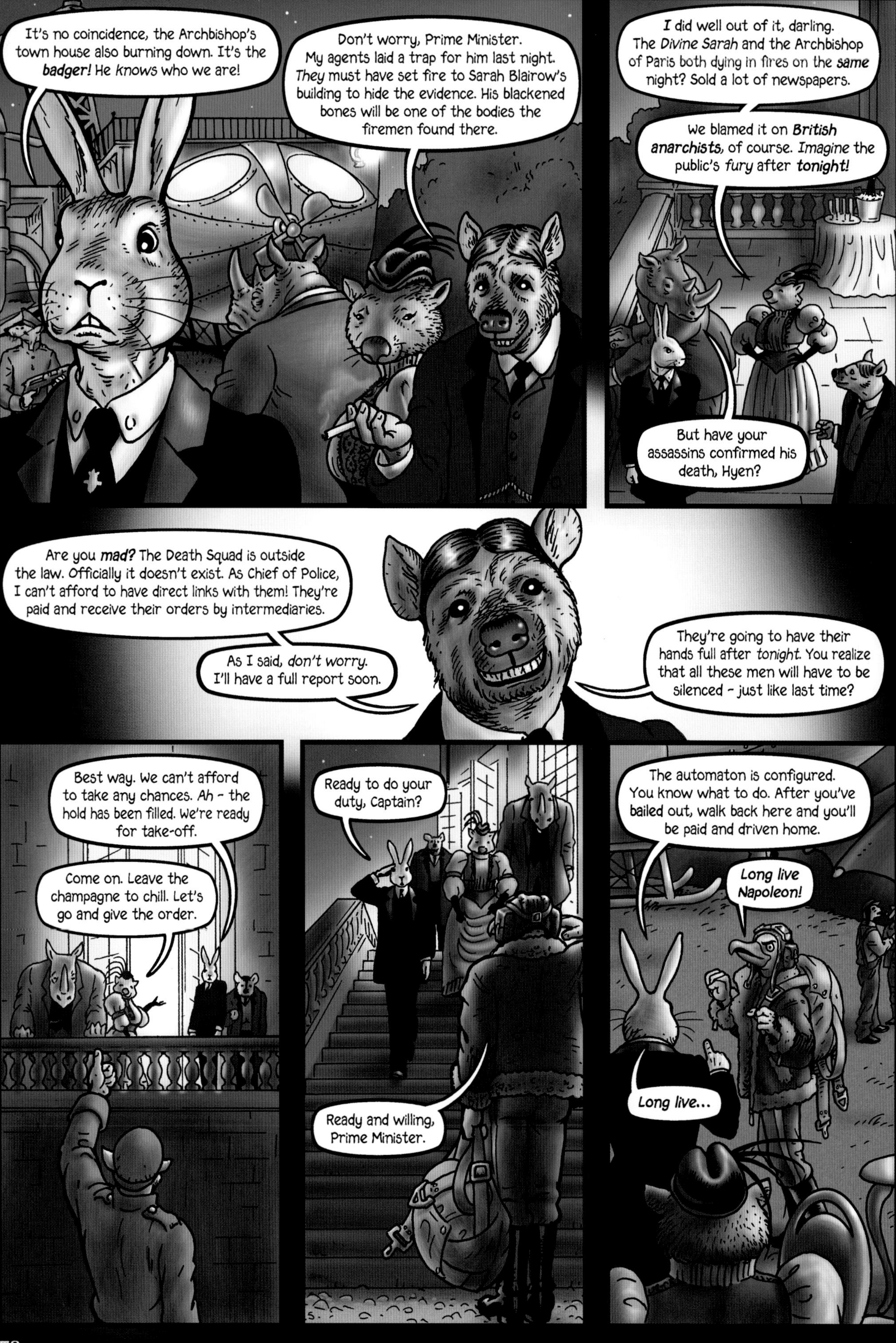
It's no coincidence, the Archbishop's town house also burning down. It's the **badger!** He *knows* who we are!
Don't worry, Prime Minister. My agents laid a trap for him last night. *They* must have set fire to Sarah Blairow's building to hide the evidence. His blackened bones will be one of the bodies the firemen found there.
I did well out of it, darling. The *Divine Sarah* and the Archbishop of Paris both dying in fires on the *same* night? Sold a lot of newspapers.
We blamed it on **British anarchists**, of course. *Imagine* the public's *fury* after **tonight!**
But have your assassins confirmed his death, Hyen?
Are you *mad?* The Death Squad is outside the law. Officially it doesn't exist. As Chief of Police, I can't afford to have direct links with them! They're paid and receive their orders by intermediaries.
As I said, *don't worry.* I'll have a full report soon.
They're going to have their hands full after *tonight.* You realize that all these men will have to be silenced - just like last time?
Best way. We can't afford to take any chances. *Ah* - the hold has been filled. We're ready for take-off.
Come on. Leave the champagne to chill. Let's go and give the order.
Ready to do your duty, Captain?
Ready and willing, Prime Minister.
The automaton is configured. You know what to do. After you've bailed out, walk back here and you'll be paid and driven home.
Long live Napoleon!
Long live...

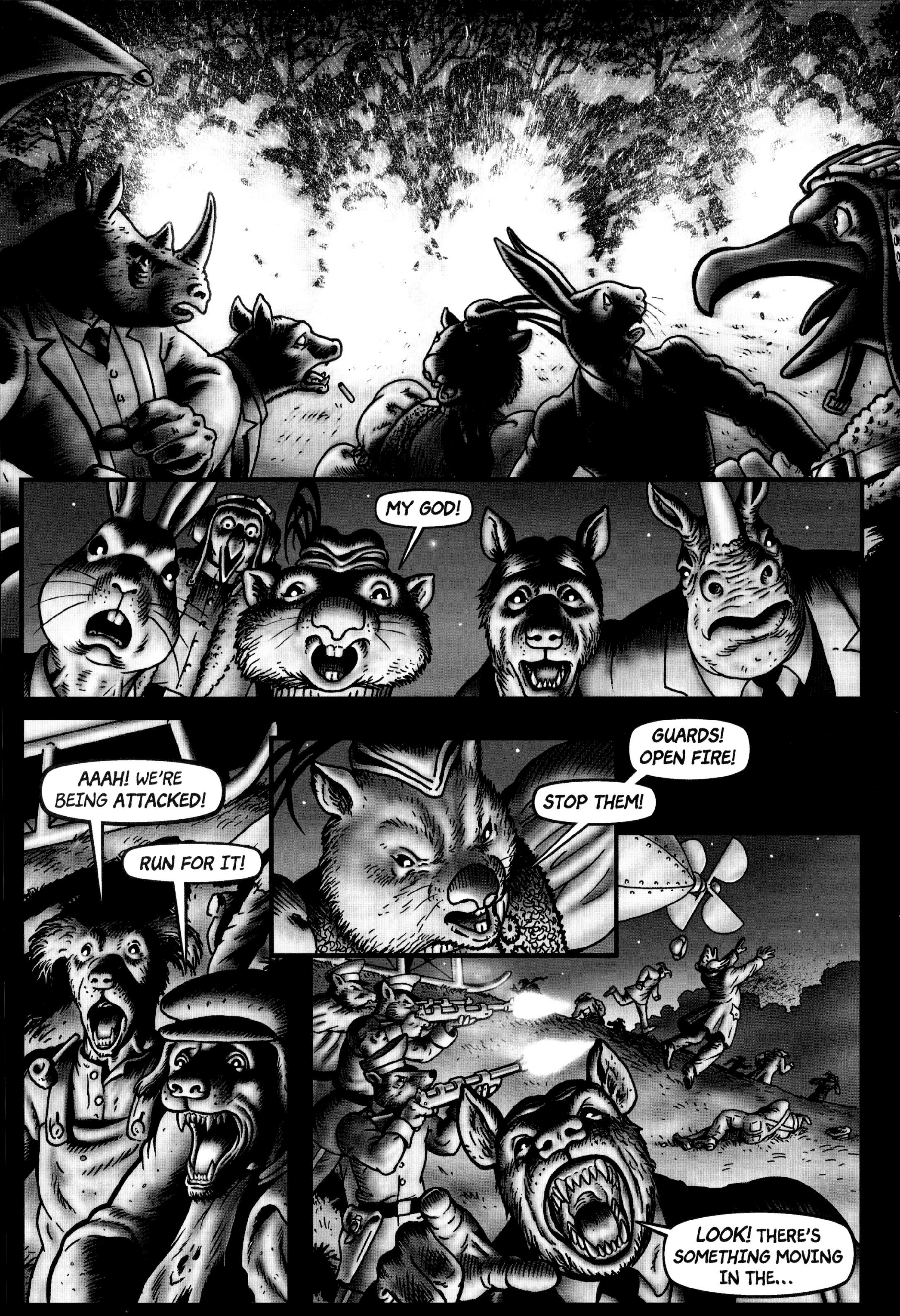
MY GOD!
AAAH! WE'RE BEING ATTACKED!
RUN FOR IT!
GUARDS! OPEN FIRE!
STOP THEM!
LOOK! THERE'S SOMETHING MOVING IN THE...

...trees.

IT'S... IT'S THE *BADGER!*
KILL HIM! KILL HIM!

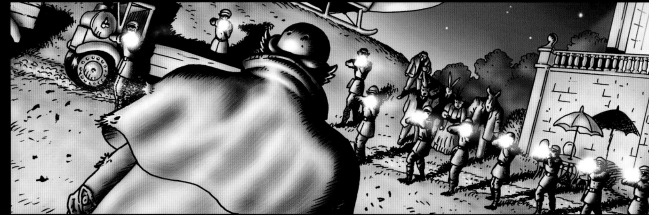

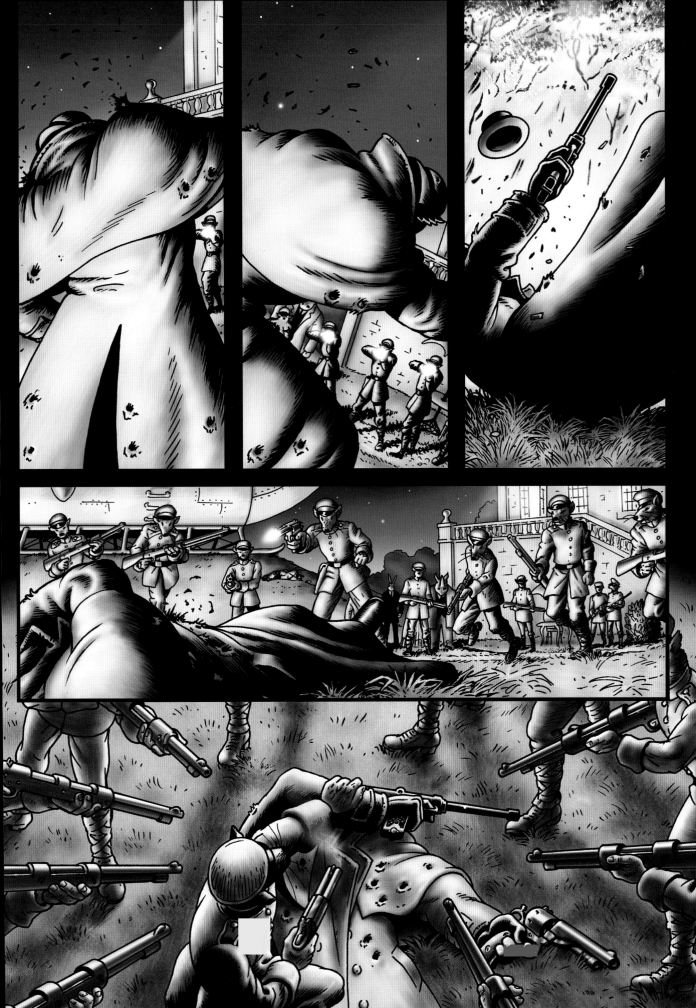

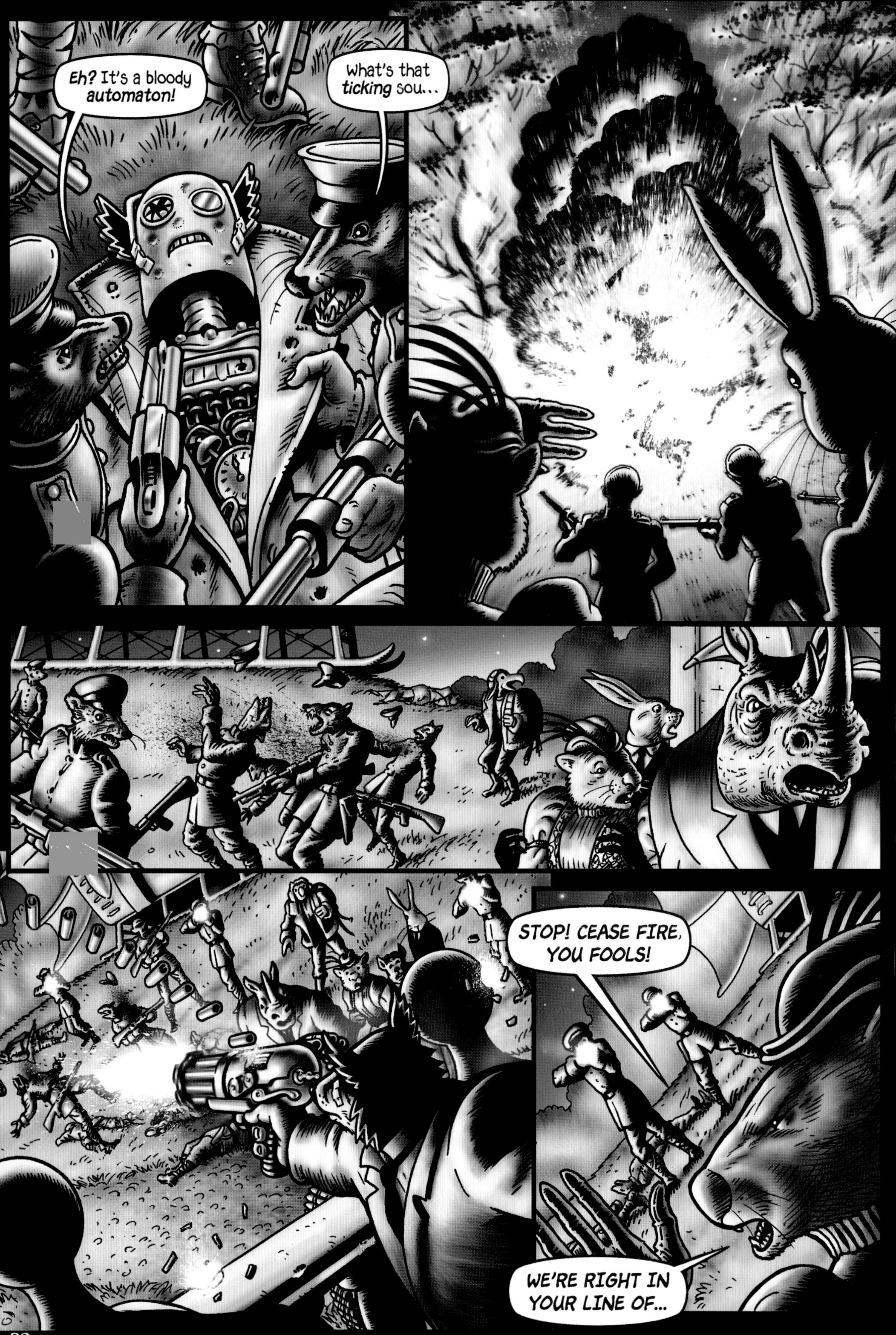
Eh? It's a bloody automaton!
What's that ticking sou...
STOP! CEASE FIRE, YOU FOOLS!
WE'RE RIGHT IN YOUR LINE OF...

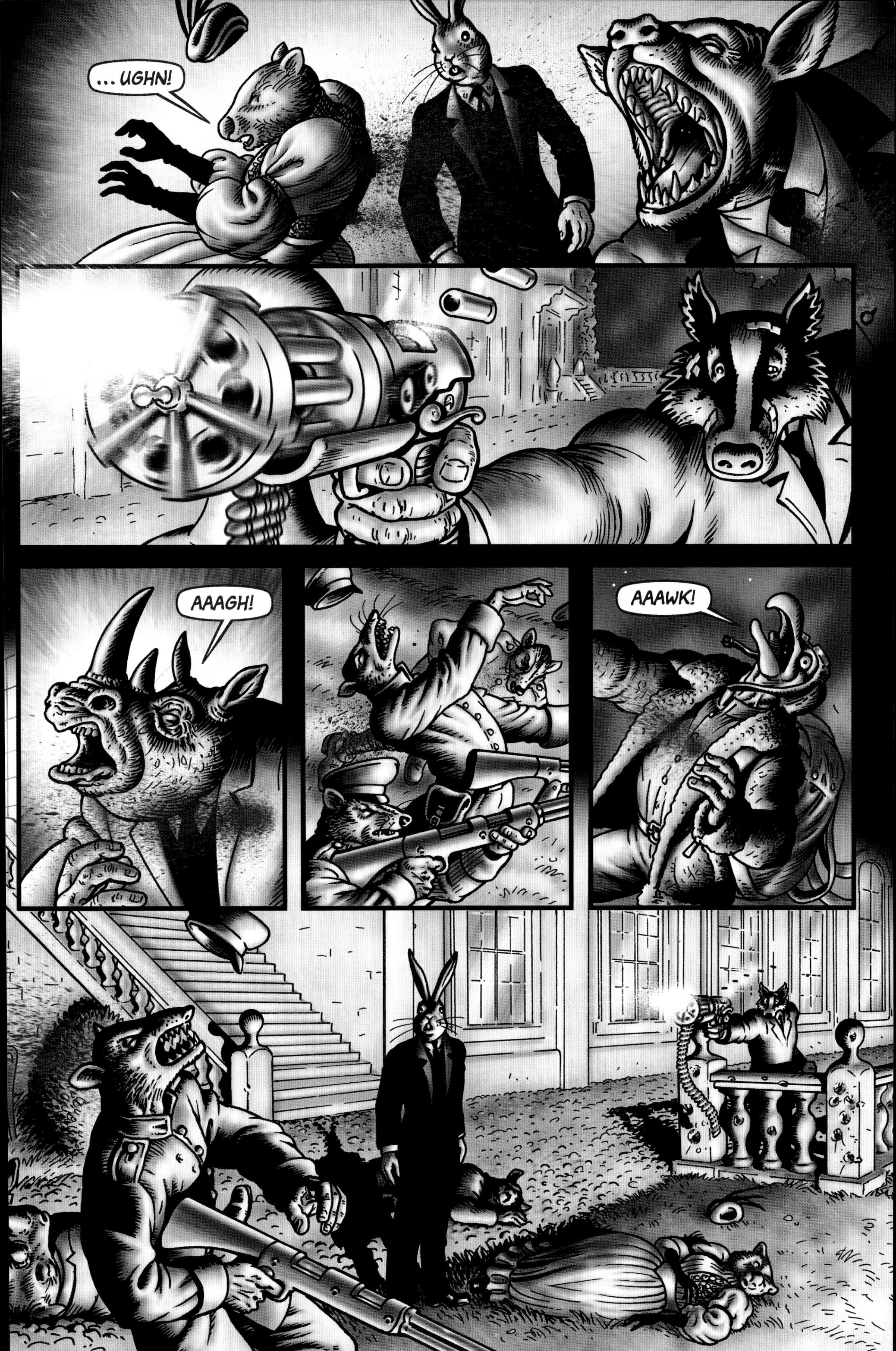
...UGHN!
AAAGH!
AAAWK!

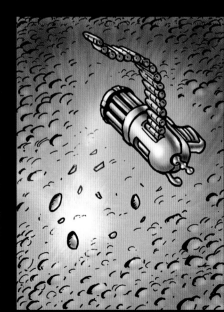

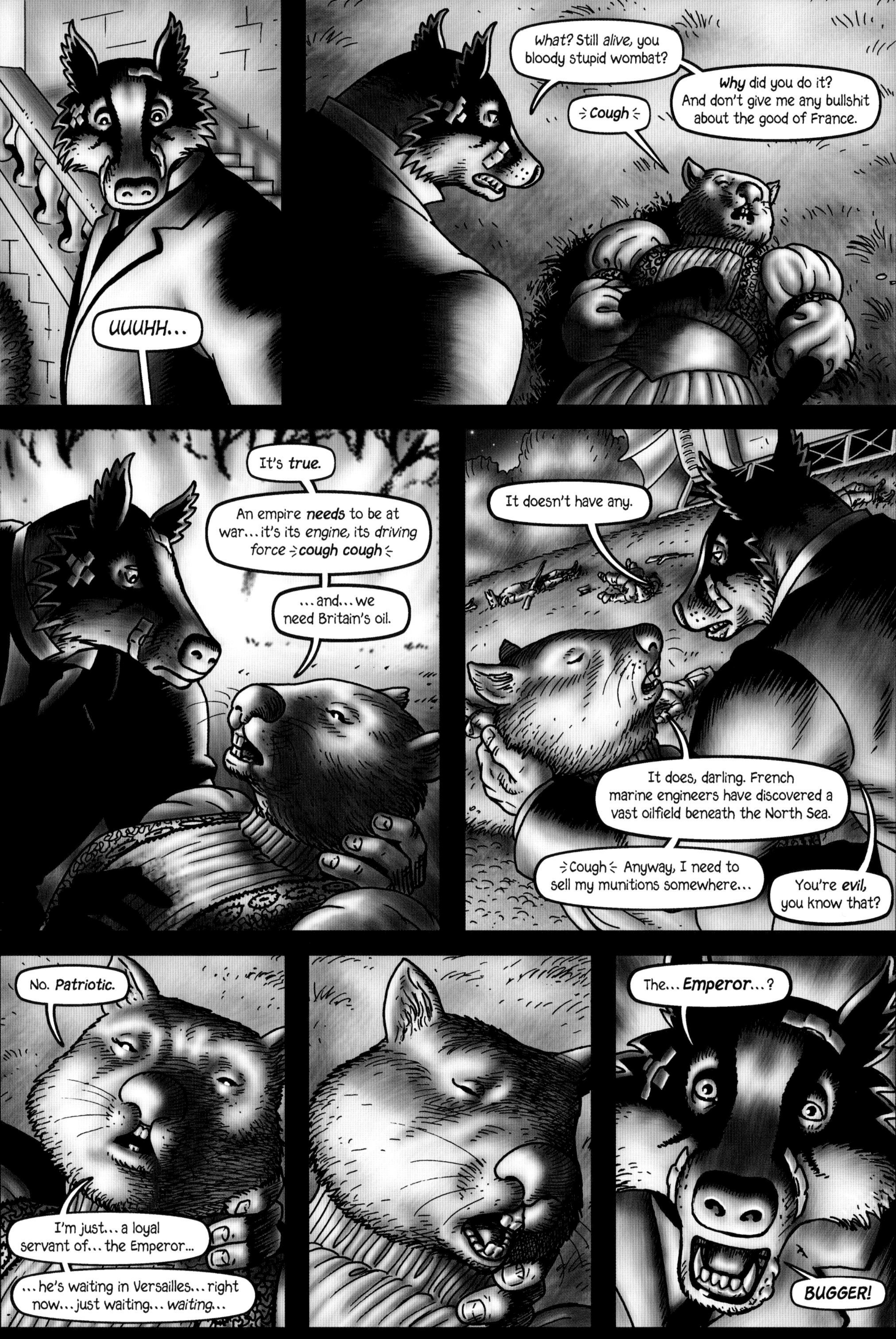
UUUHH...
What? Still *alive*, you bloody stupid wombat?
⩥ **Cough** ⩤
Why did you do it? And don't give me any bullshit about the good of France.
It's **true**.
An empire **needs** to be at war... it's its *engine*, its *driving force* ⩥ **cough cough** ⩤
...and... we need Britain's oil.
It doesn't have any.
It does, darling. French marine engineers have discovered a vast oilfield beneath the North Sea.
⩥ Cough ⩤ Anyway, I need to sell my munitions somewhere...
You're **evil**, you know that?
No. **Patriotic**.
I'm just... a loyal servant of... the Emperor...
...he's waiting in Versailles... right now... just waiting... *waiting*...
The... **Emperor**...?
BUGGER!

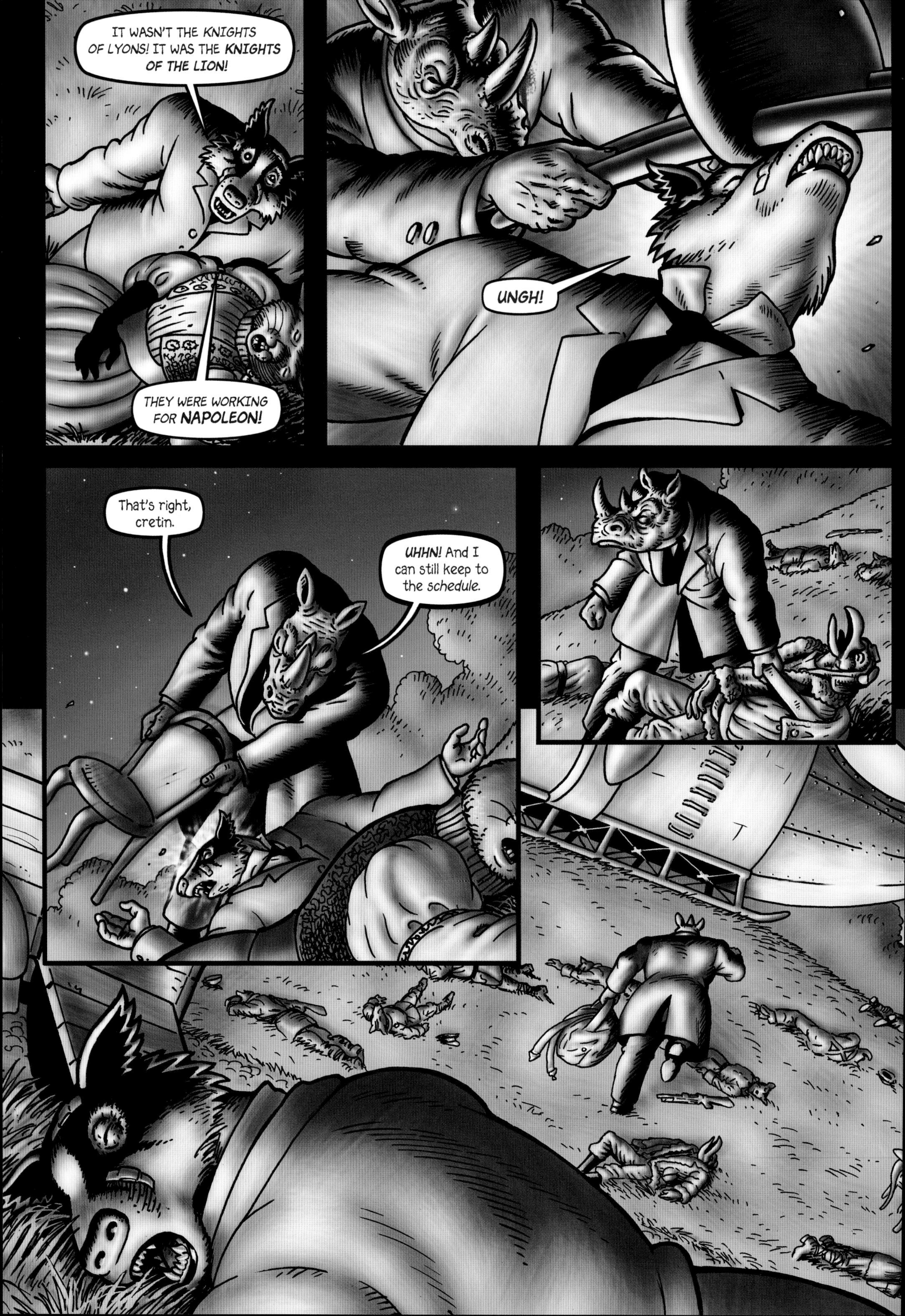
IT WASN'T THE KNIGHTS OF LYONS! IT WAS THE KNIGHTS OF THE LION!
THEY WERE WORKING FOR NAPOLEON!
UNGH!
That's right, cretin.
UHHN! And I can still keep to the schedule.

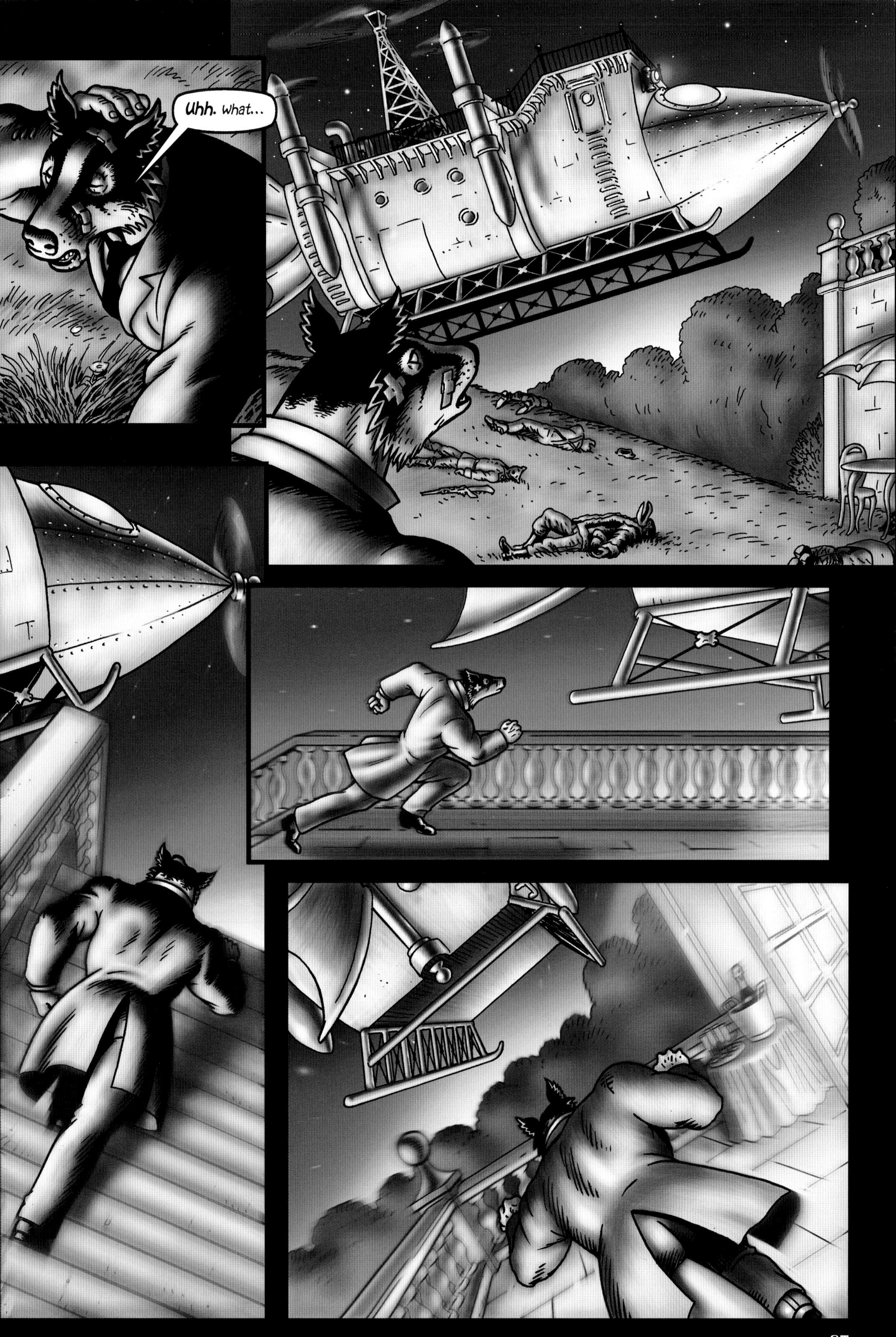
Uhh. what...

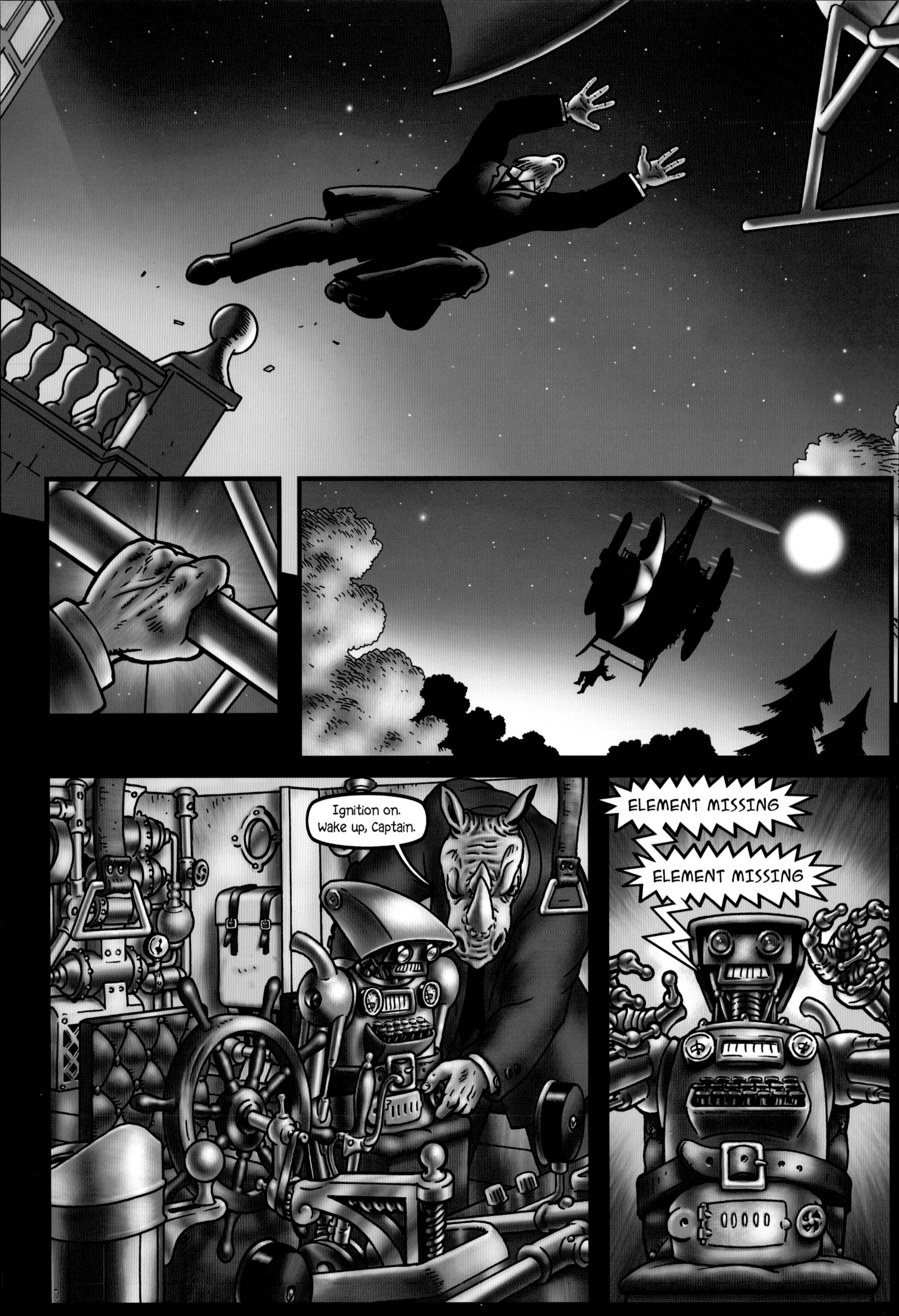
Ignition on. Wake up, Captain.
ELEMENT MISSING
ELEMENT MISSING

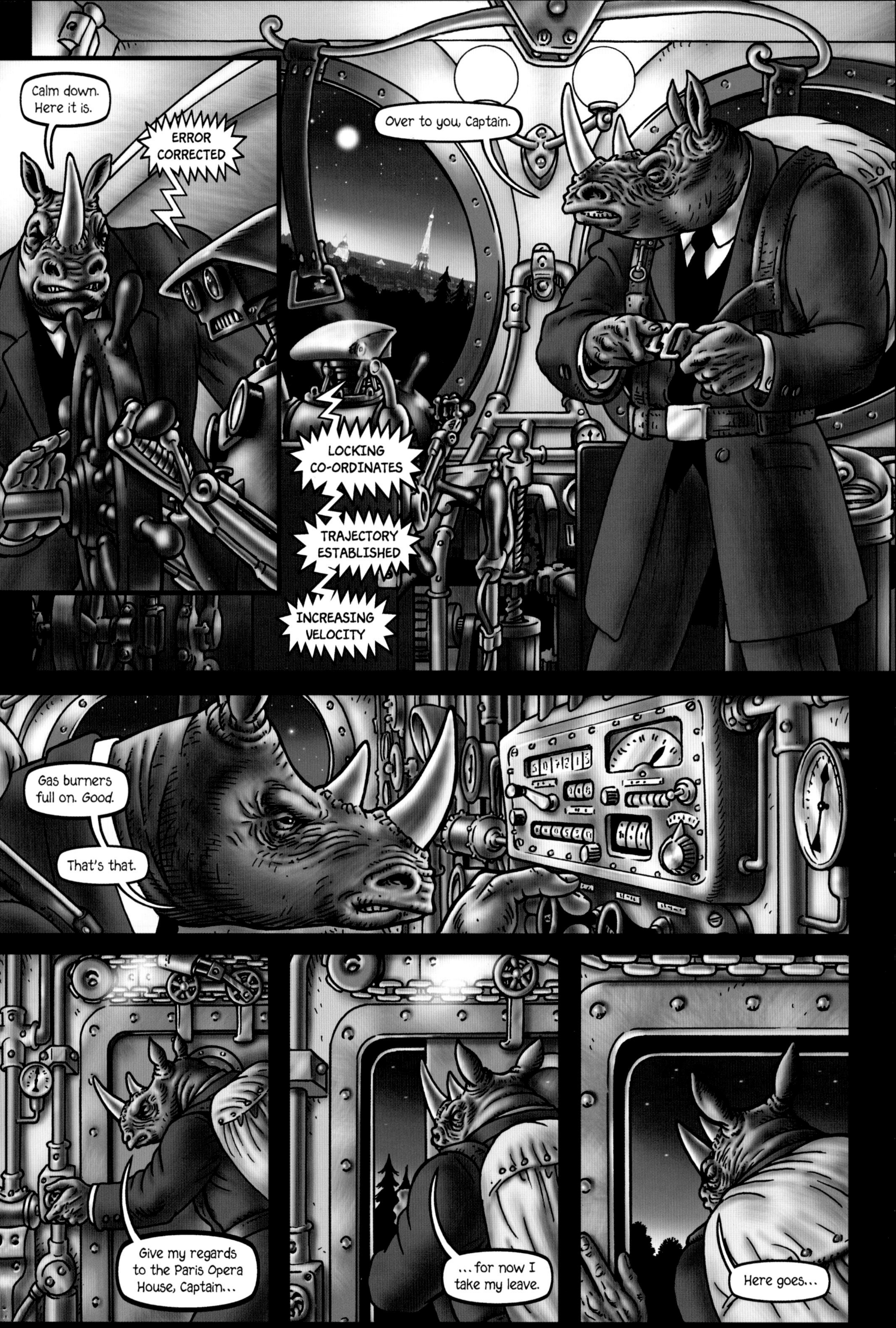
Calm down. Here it is.
ERROR CORRECTED
Over to you, Captain.
LOCKING CO-ORDINATES
TRAJECTORY ESTABLISHED
INCREASING VELOCITY
Gas burners full on. *Good.*
That's that.
Give my regards to the Paris Opera House, Captain...
...for now I take my leave.
Here goes...

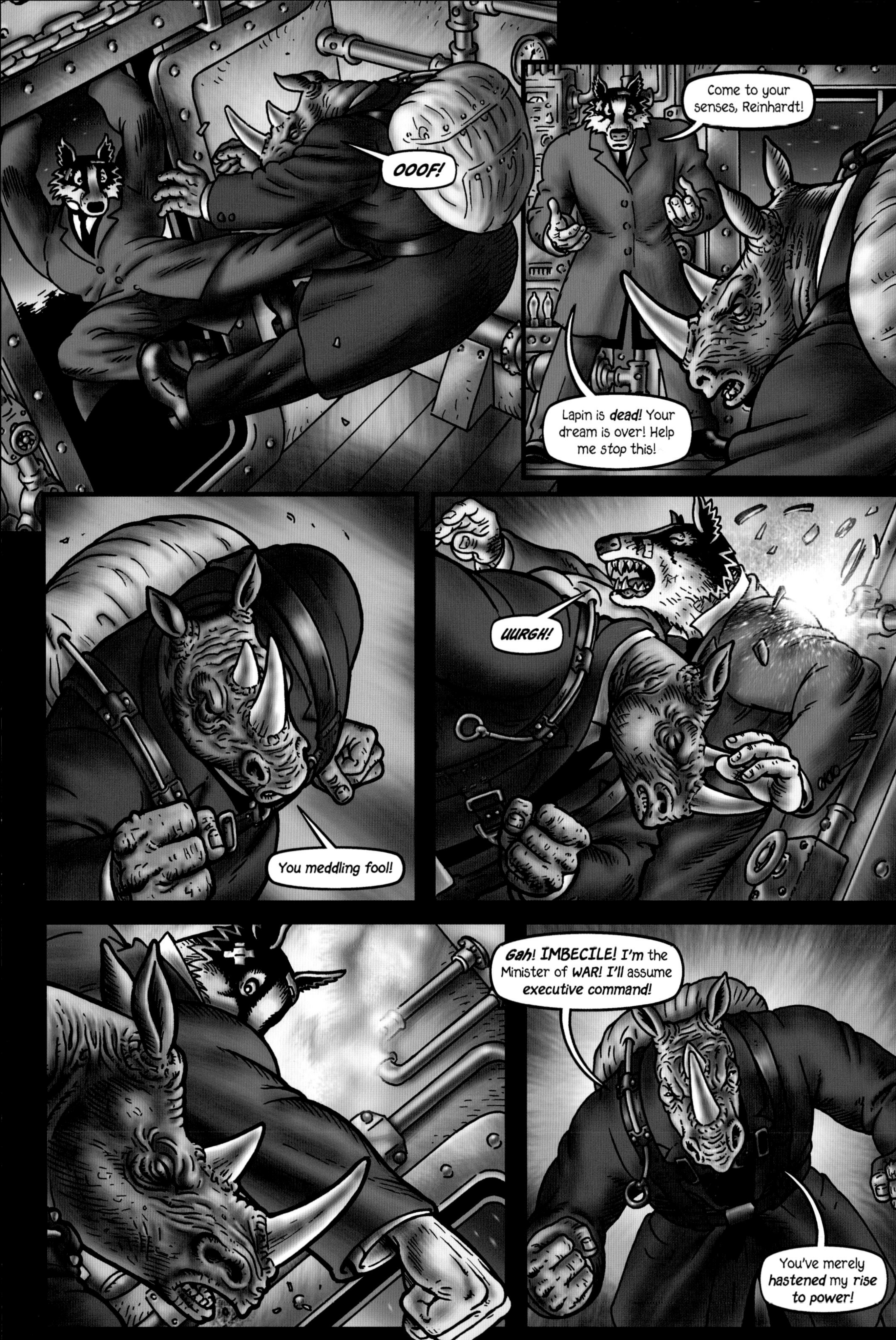
OOOF!
Come to your senses, Reinhardt!
Lapin is *dead!* Your dream is over! Help me *stop* this!
You meddling fool!
UURGH!
Gah! **IMBECILE!** I'm the Minister of ***WAR! I'll*** assume ***executive command!***
You've merely ***hastened*** my ***rise to power!***

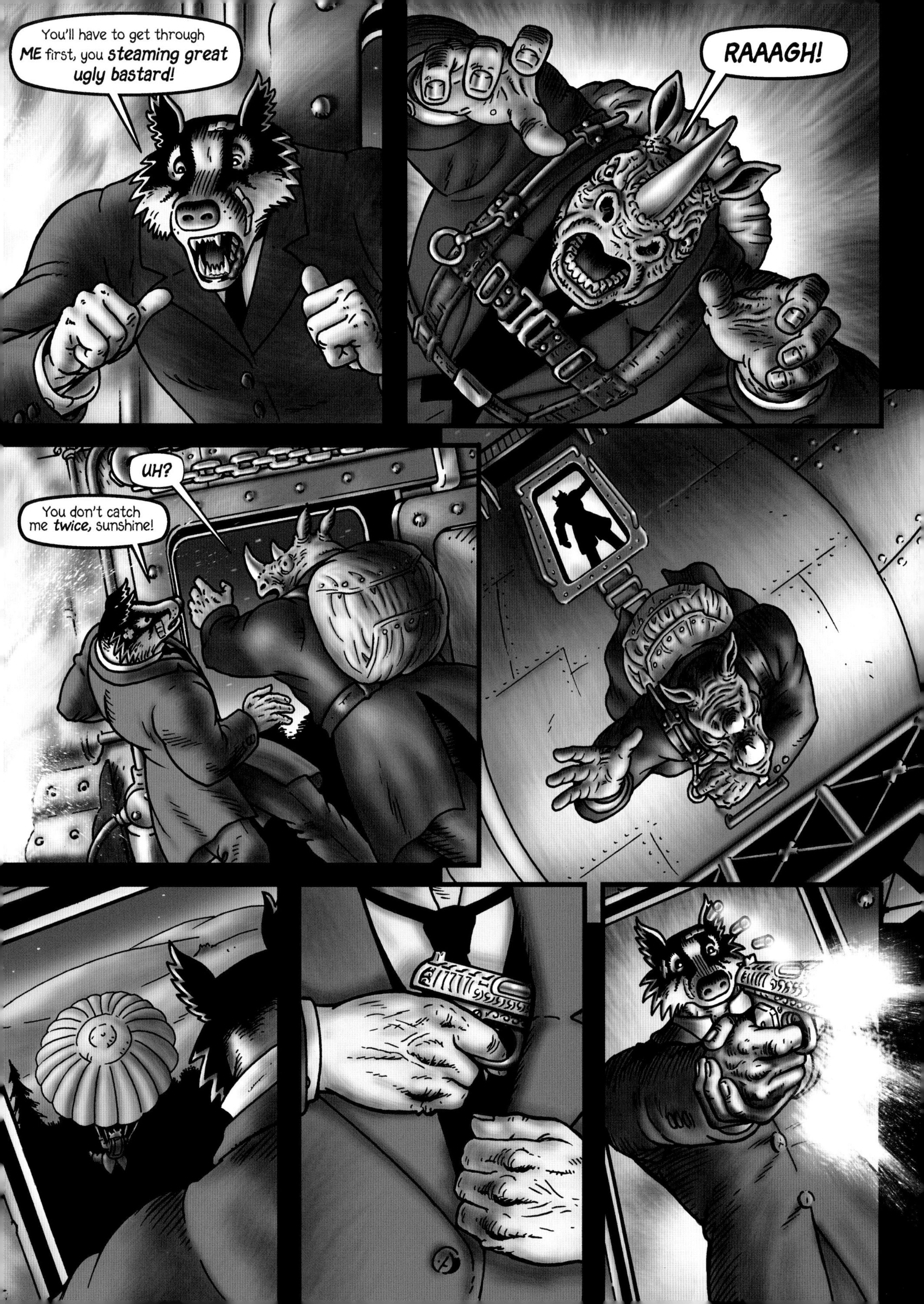
You'll have to get through ME first, you steaming great ugly bastard!
RAAAGH!
UH?
You don't catch me twice, sunshine!

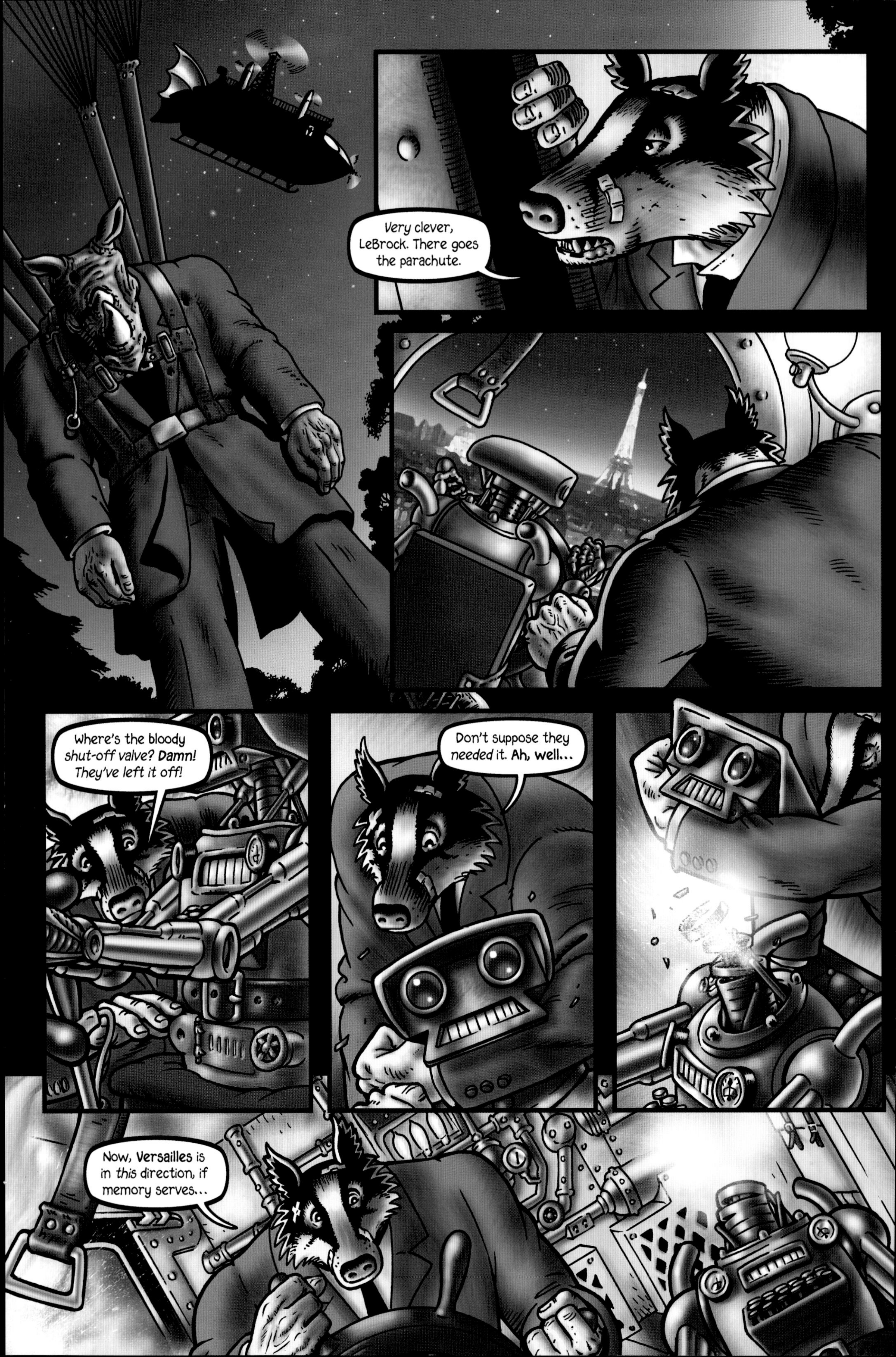
Very clever, LeBrock. There goes the parachute.
Where's the bloody shut-off valve? Damn! They've left it off!
Don't suppose they needed it. Ah, well...
Now, Versailles is in this direction, if memory serves...

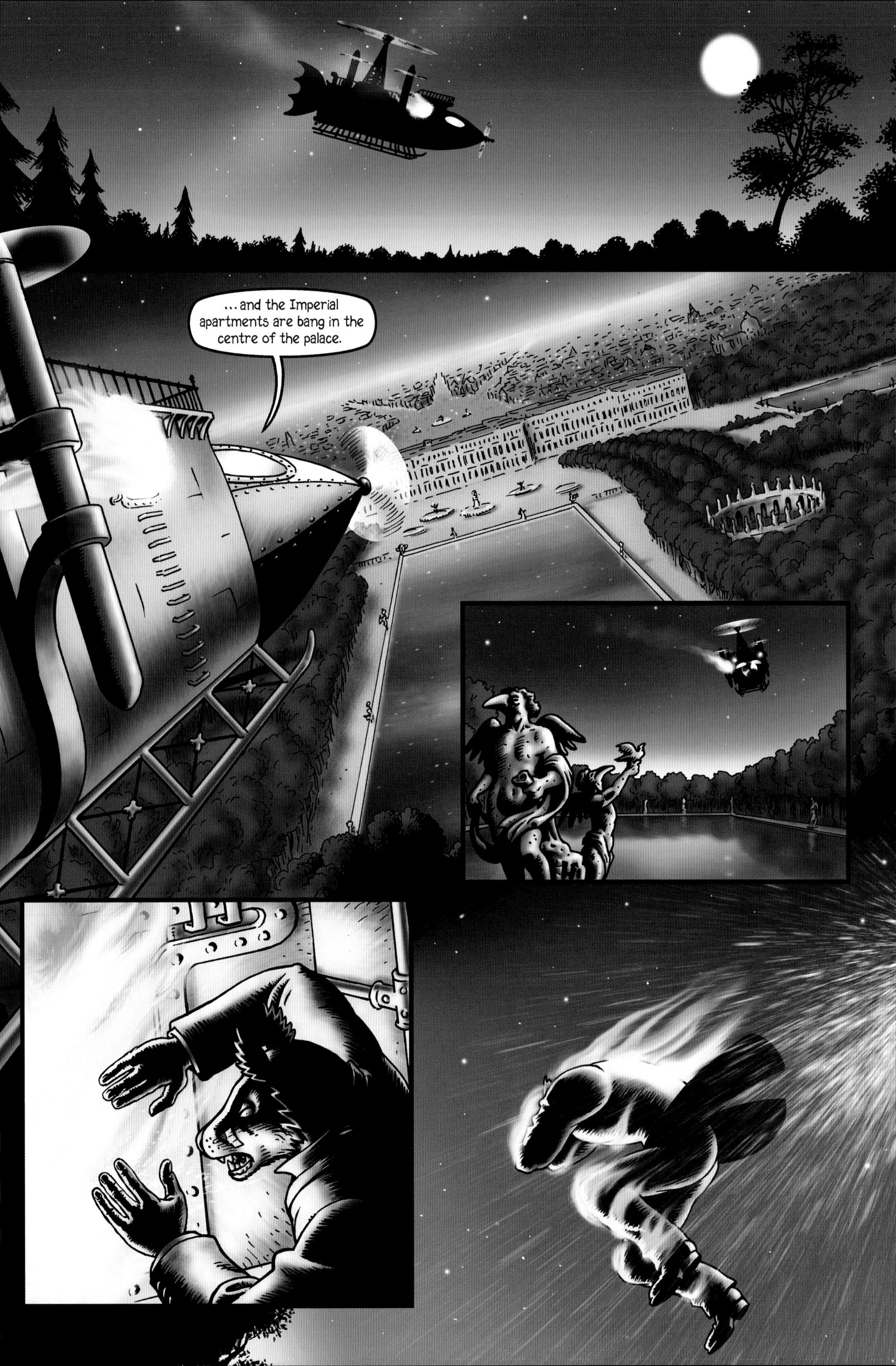
...and the Imperial apartments are bang in the centre of the palace.

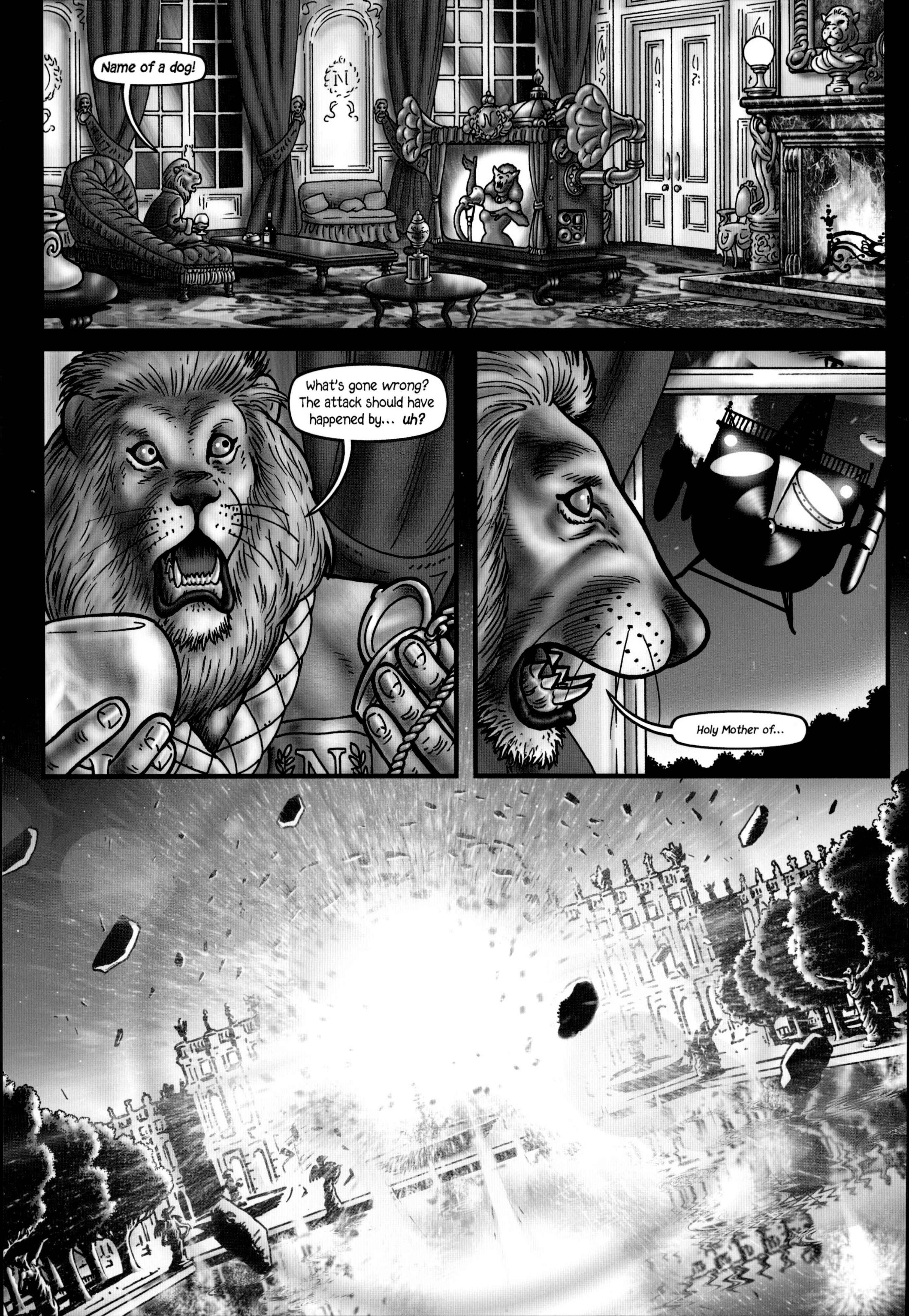
Name of a dog!
What's gone wrong? The attack should have happened by... uh?
Holy Mother of...

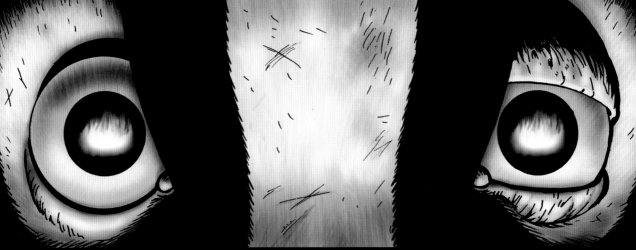

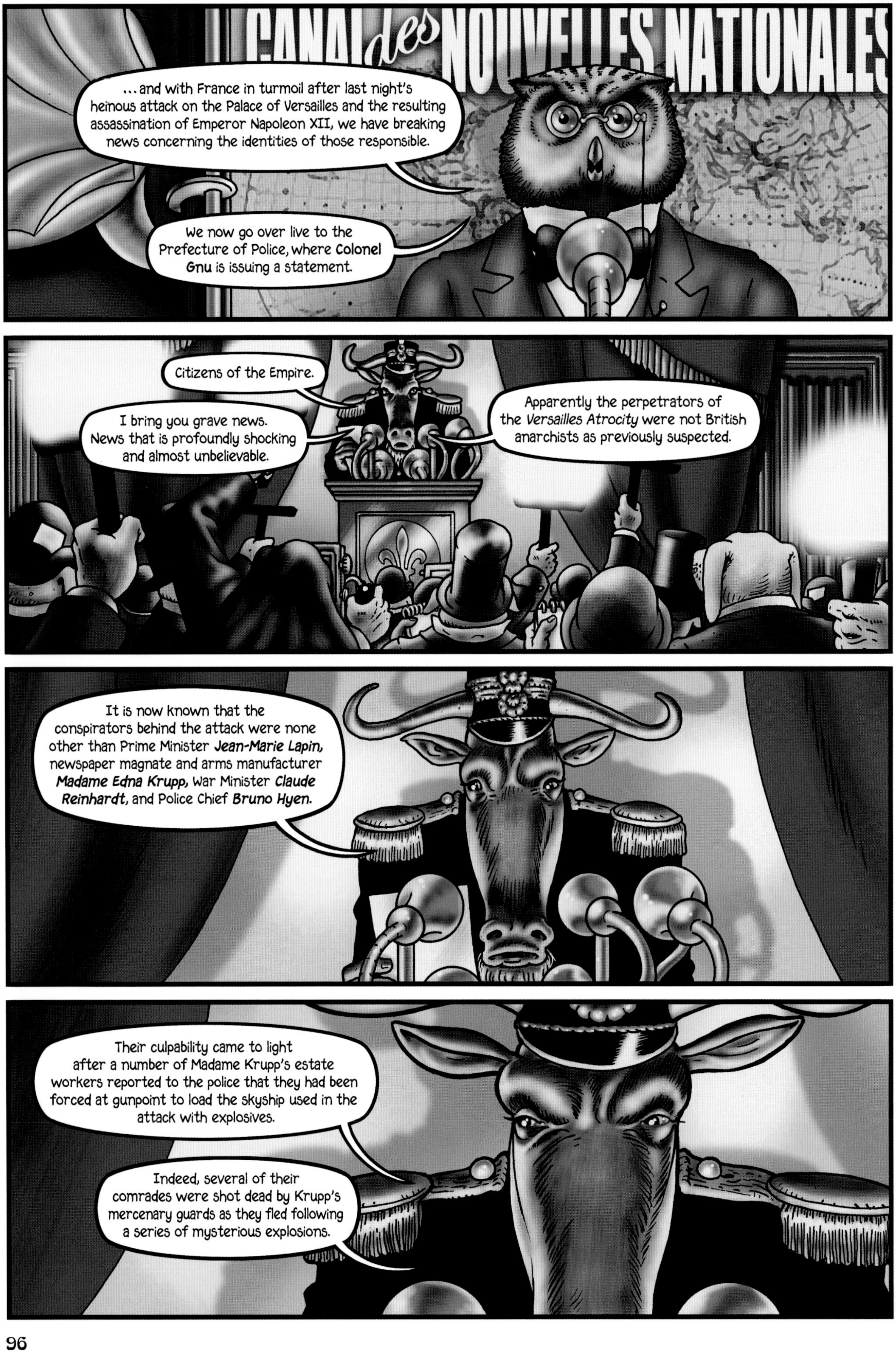
CANAL des NOUVELLES NATIONALES
...and with France in turmoil after last night's heinous attack on the Palace of Versailles and the resulting assassination of Emperor Napoleon XII, we have breaking news concerning the identities of those responsible.
We now go over live to the Prefecture of Police, where **Colonel Gnu** is issuing a statement.
Citizens of the Empire.
I bring you grave news. News that is profoundly shocking and almost unbelievable.
Apparently the perpetrators of the *Versailles Atrocity* were not British anarchists as previously suspected.
It is now known that the conspirators behind the attack were none other than Prime Minister ***Jean-Marie Lapin,*** newspaper magnate and arms manufacturer ***Madame Edna Krupp,*** War Minister ***Claude Reinhardt,*** and Police Chief ***Bruno Hyen.***
Their culpability came to light after a number of Madame Krupp's estate workers reported to the police that they had been forced at gunpoint to load the skyship used in the attack with explosives.
Indeed, several of their comrades were shot dead by Krupp's mercenary guards as they fled following a series of mysterious explosions.

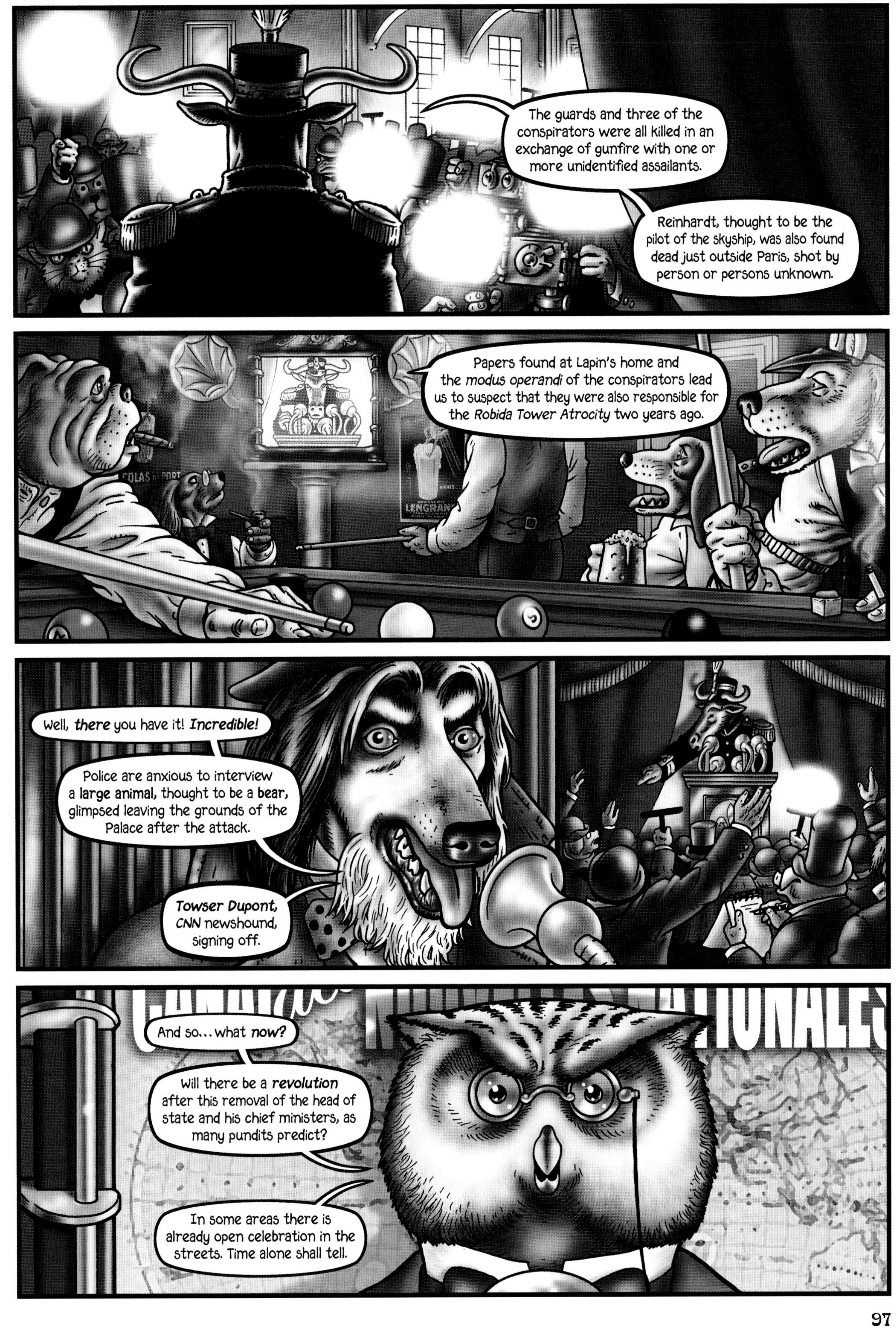
The guards and three of the conspirators were all killed in an exchange of gunfire with one or more unidentified assailants.
Reinhardt, thought to be the pilot of the skyship, was also found dead just outside Paris, shot by person or persons unknown.
Papers found at Lapin's home and the *modus operandi* of the conspirators lead us to suspect that they were also responsible for the *Robida Tower Atrocity* two years ago.
Well, **there** you have it! ***Incredible!***
Police are anxious to interview a **large animal,** thought to be a **bear,** glimpsed leaving the grounds of the Palace after the attack.
Towser Dupont, CNN newshound, signing off.
And so... what ***now?***
Will there be a ***revolution*** after this removal of the head of state and his chief ministers, as many pundits predict?
In some areas there is already open celebration in the streets. Time alone shall tell.

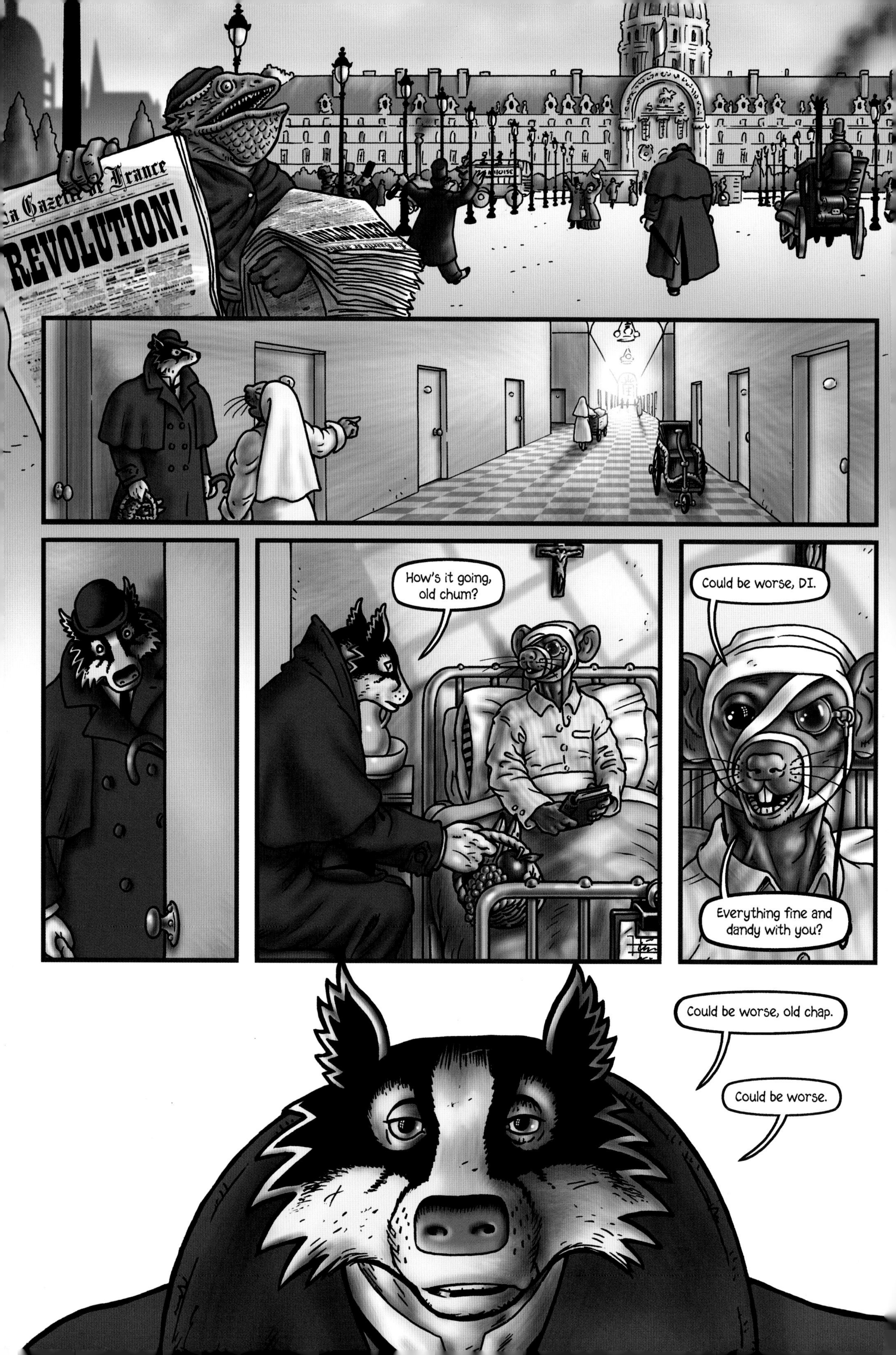
La Gazette de France
REVOLUTION!
How's it going, old chum?
Could be worse, DI.
Everything fine and dandy with you?
Could be worse, old chap.
Could be worse.

GRANDVILLE

Fin

publication design
BRYAN TALBOT

publisher
MIKE RICHARDSON

editor
CHRIS WARNER

GRANDVILLE™

Dark Horse Books
A division of Dark Horse Comics, Inc.
10956 S.E. Main Street
Milwaukie OR 97222

darkhorse.com

To find a comics shop in your area, call the Comic Shop Locator Service toll-free at 1-888-266-4226

First edition: October 2009
ISBN 978-1-59582-397-7

10 9 8 7 6 5 4 3 2
Printed at 1010 Printing International, Ltd., Guangdong Province, China.

Other books by Bryan Talbot

Brainstorm!
The Adventures of Luther Arkwright
Heart of Empire
The Tale of One Bad Rat
Alice in Sunderland
The Art of Bryan Talbot
The Naked Artist (Prose)
Grandville Mon Amour
Metronome

(Writing as Veronique Tanaka)

Cherubs!

(With Mark Stafford)

Nemesis the Warlock Vols 1 & 2

(With Pat Mills)

Sandman: Fables and Reflections

(With Neil Gaiman, Stan Woch & Mark Buckingham)

The Dead Boy Detectives and
the Secret of Immortality

(With Ed Brubaker & Steve Leialoha)

www.bryan-talbot.com

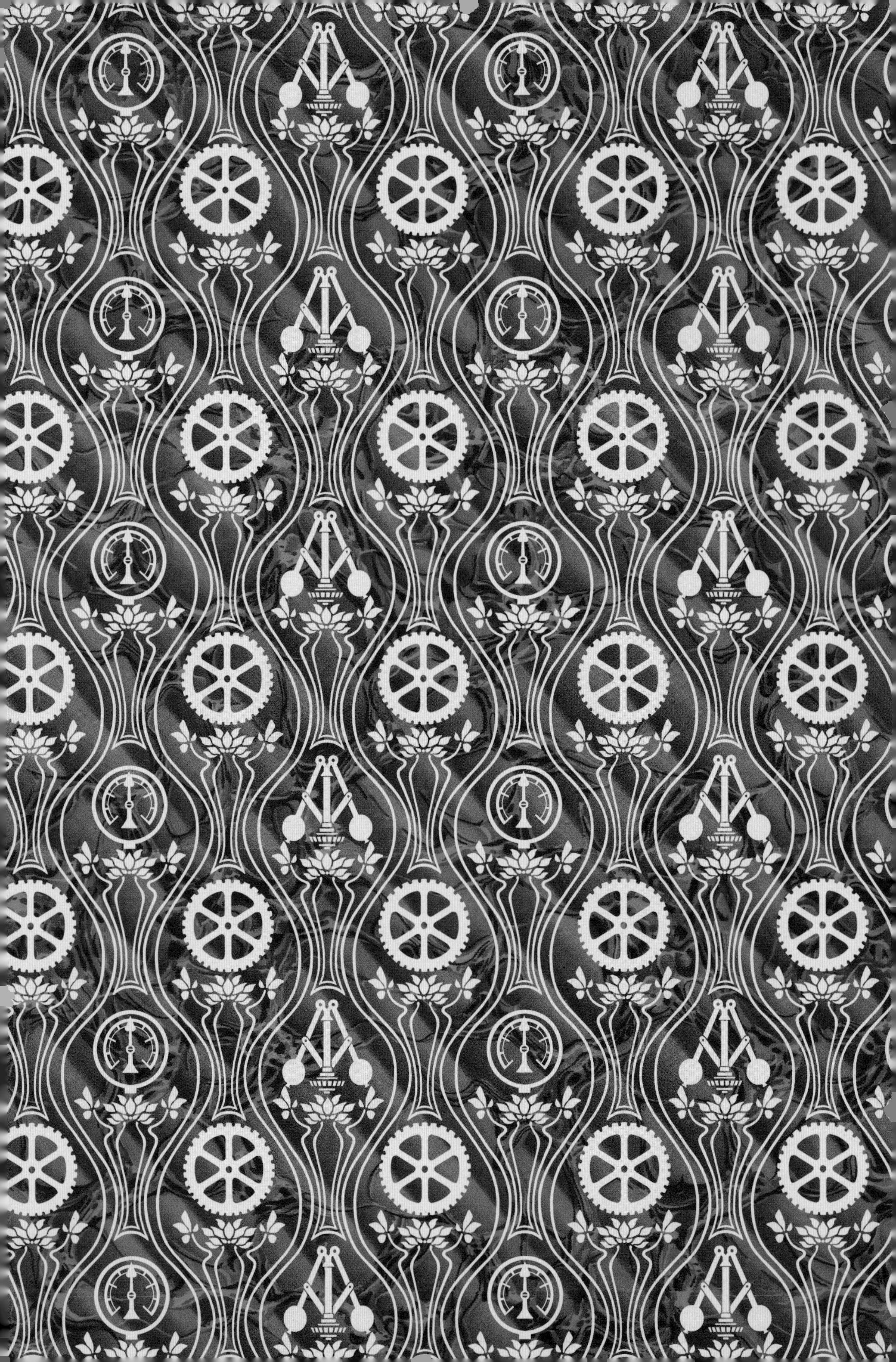